D1552535

LEADING IN CRISIS TIMES

The Art of Turning Setbacks into Comebacks

DR. KEITH JOHNSON

The Confidence Coach

LEADING IN CRISIS TIMES

The Art of Turning Setbacks into Comebacks
© Copyright 2010 by Keith Johnson, PhD
All rights reserved.

ISBN:

ISBN: 0-9662283-9-1

Printed in The U.S.A.

Cover Artwork, Illustrations, and Interior Layout by:
Palm Tree Productions—*www.palmtreeproductions.net*

To contact the author or order more resources:

www.DrKeithJohnson.com

CONTENTS

Other books by
Keith Johnson, Ph.D.

**The Confidence Makeover – How to
Create the New and Confidence You**

The Confidence Makeover Journal

Ten Habits of Highly Confident People

**Leaders of Destiny – The Art of
Turning Dreams into Reality**

Coaching For Results

INTRODUCTION

The World is in Crisis

Almost every global institution—economic, religious, education, environmental, employment, political, military—is facing a major crisis these days.

To get out of these crises, confident leaders must step forward and lead their organization through them. The current financial crisis in the United States was not caused by subprime mortgages, credit default swaps, or failed economic policies. The root cause was and continues to be failed leadership. The problems we face today as a nation, state, community, business, and even churches can be solved only by raising up new leaders with the confidence, competence, and character needed to put things back on the right course of action.

This is your opportunity. You can make a difference!

A single voice can change the world. Whether the voice speaks out against terrorism, provides solutions to our current economic troubles, describes a new scientific invention, discovers a new medical breakthrough, tells a story, releases spiritual truths, or speaks of a previously voiceless generation, a voice can reach across national borders and into future generations to transform the world that follows.

Great changes have occurred in the past 100 years. Many of the voices of the 20th century have passed away—and history books are waiting to be written about the new voices that God will use in this generation. Who will He use to change the world? It may be you.

Many new voices may be currently facing tremendous trials, setbacks, and crises. They may even be voted "less likely to succeed" at this stage in their lives. However, a crisis is actually a launching pad to success and a doorway to promotion. F. Scott Fitzgerald said, "Show me a hero, and I will write you a tragedy."

In time of crises, a true leader will emerge. In every generation, there comes a time when a leader must come forward to meet the needs of the hour. Whether it is your greatest hour or your worst, is up to you.

Real success is doing something in this life that will impact generations to come. You must refuse to leave this earth without leaving some kind of legacy. Mark Twain said, "Let us endeavor to live that when we come to die even the undertaker will be sorry."

Developing a powerful impact in this world starts by boldly renouncing a quiet, mediocre, small thinking, low-impact life. This is the beginning of becoming all that God wants you to be.

I hope this book will help you fulfill your dreams. The best days of your life are ahead of you.

Stay confident!

CHAPTER ONE

CRISIS: THE CLASSROOM

Seeds of greatness are inside every human being, and sometimes it takes a crisis to expose them. A crisis forces you out of your comfort zone!

"What will it take for you to change your attitude and fulfill your potential—to move out of your comfort zone?" These words were spoken to me one day by the Holy Spirit. Whenever the Holy Spirit asks you a question, the best thing to do is to play stupid! Why? Because He already knows the answer. To me, this was an important question that continues to challenge me every day of my life.

God longs to use you. He has a great purpose and destiny for your life. Jesus came to deliver you from failure and to make you an effective and successful person. If you remain who you are, you will never become all God wants you to be. Therefore, you must take steps toward radically changing who you are. The time to start is now! The stakes are high. Thousands of lives are awaiting your arrival into your destiny.

There is one thing that I have learned about human beings: we hate change. We prefer to stay nice and cozy in our daily routines. The only human beings I have found who truly like change are babies with wet diapers. We may know we need to change and we probably sincerely want to change, but we naturally try to avoid change when at all possible.

The world changes every day. George Barna in his book, *The Second Coming of the Church* says, "Our society is reinventing itself every three to five years." I can assure you of one thing, change will happen! The business world knows that if a company does not change with the times and embrace new technology they will go bankrupt over a period of time.

Better than Average

The only organization that thinks it can remain the same and still be effective is the church. The Christian message will always be relevant and life-changing. Why? Because every individual deep down inside longs to be different. Everybody wants an instant "makeover." When you accept Jesus Christ, you receive the greatest makeover you have ever experienced. When He comes in, depression goes out! When He comes in, your life will radically change. Our message must always remain the same, but the methods of how we present the gospel must change.

When I share the message of change with people worldwide, they ask, "I thought God loved me just the way I am?" Yes, God does love you just the way you are, and no amount of work can cause Him to love you more. God also loves you so much that He refuses to allow you to remain who you are. He does not want you to be average or like the status quo. *Average* and *good* are the enemies of *God's best!*

You were created to achieve something great and significant for the Kingdom of God. Ordinary people become extraordinary when they decide to change and be different. Only extraordinary people achieve extraordinary things. You were called to be effective, to carry out exploits, and to do something extraordinary with your life.

> *"...but the people who know their God shall*
> *be strong, and carry out **great exploits.***
>
> —*Daniel 11:32*
> (Emphasis Added)

Therefore, God wants to move you out of your comfort zone of *average*, and place you in His classroom to teach, mature, build, and prepare you to be a better and stronger person than you are today.

Methods of Change

How do you change, and what causes you to move out of your comfort zone? The Bible teaches us that change takes place by three different methods:

METHOD 1: You are changed in the presence of God (see 2 Cor. 3:17). True transformation takes place when you have had a personal encounter with the Creator of the universe. You will never be truly changed in the presence of people— only in the presence of God. But it is also possible for a person to be in the presence of God and not be changed. After all, Lucifer and Judas were in the very presence of God but didn't change from their evil and deceitful ways.

METHOD 2: You are changed by the renewing of your mind. *"And do not be conformed to this world, but be transformed by the renewing of your mind, that you may prove what is that good and acceptable and perfect will of God"* (Romans 12:2). It is also possible for you to continually learn new truth, but never change your actions.

METHOD 3: You experience change when you experience a crisis. Hundreds of books have been written about the first two methods, but very few books have been written about how a crisis can be an instrument of change.

Dr. Mark Chironna says, "In the pursuit of your life's purpose, there will strategically occur a defining moment in the form of a refining crisis setting you free from a confining limitation, thus empowering you to step into greatness."[1]

If you refuse to change, the Lord will supernaturally orchestrate certain circumstances in your life to get you where He wants you to be. In His love, God will allow you to walk through a crisis, trial, or even experience a setback. This will cause you to move into a season of process, evaluation, and change. After the process is over, I believe and have witnessed, that God will supernaturally promote you if you change and pass the test.

When I look back over my life, I realize that there was a process that I had to go through in order for me to change different areas in my life. It took a tragic motorcycle accident while I was in college to get me out of a drunken college fraternity. That crisis led me to Florida where I would eventually meet my wife and give my heart and life to Jesus Christ.

It took a financial crisis before I would accept God's laws of prosperity by giving tithes and offerings. I also faced a marriage crisis that caused me to dig for more information about how to properly treat and love my wife. I discovered a great new truth, if I want to be treated like a king, I better start treating my wife like a queen. After all, every queen needs a king!

The Time to Change is Now

One of the saddest crises that I faced in my personal life was when my father had a sudden heart attack and died. After I had given my life to Jesus Christ, Dad and I had a very hard time getting along. He liked to party, and he drank beer continuously. Our relationship was so bad that we hadn't talked to each other in years. When my dad suddenly died, I no longer had the chance to restore the relationship.

There were things I wanted to tell him, one last hug to give him, and one more plea for his salvation. I wanted to talk to him about all the good times we had together when I was a kid; days when he took me to work with him, camping and fishing trips, and times we shared talking to one another. I wanted to tell him one last time, "Dad, I will always love you," but now it's too late.

This crisis caused me to move into a process of evaluation. I embraced change and decided that I needed to change my attitude toward other family members. I have worked hard at restoring these relationships. Now I realize that time spent with family is very important. Why? Because they will not be around forever.

I faced another crisis when I went through a season of burnout in the ministry. The crisis caused me to change my "one man show, superstar mentality" thinking to grasping the concept of team ministry.

Man is not imprisoned by habit.
Great changes in him can be wrought by crisis—
once that crisis can be recognized and understood.

—*Norman Cousins*[2]

A crisis can also come when you are walking in the perfect will of God. What we may call a crisis, God calls a classroom. I know there are some preachers out there who will tell you that if you are really walking with God, you will not face any problems. This is simply not the truth.

The Bible is full of illustrations of powerful men and women of God who faced great persecutions and trials while doing the will of God. The apostle Peter taught us that crisis is a normal occurrence on the road to fulfilling the will of God for our lives, *"Beloved, do not think it strange concerning the fiery trial which is to try you, as though some strange thing happened to you"* (1 Peter 4:12).

Jesus Christ also taught us the same truth when He says in John, *"...These things I have spoken to you, that in Me you may have peace. In the world **you will have tribulation**; but be of good cheer, I have overcome the world"* (John 16:33). Jesus went through some crises, trials, and persecutions to learn obedience, *"though He was a Son, yet He **learned** obedience by the things which He **suffered**"* (Hebrews 5:8). If you have not faced any storms in your life, then you are not attempting to accomplish anything significant for the Kingdom of God.

There is a three-step process that every person walks through in life *before they can experience divine promotion:*

STEP 1—THE CRISIS: A crisis can come from four different avenues: yourself, the devil, another person's bad decision, or natural circumstances and even doing the will of God for your life. The crisis moves you out of your comfort zone and into a process of change.

STEP 2—THE PROCESS: You embrace change, learn new truth, work on your weaknesses, and prepare yourself to step into supernatural promotion.

STEP 3—THE PROMOTION: The result of every crisis should end in supernatural promotion and victory. The process has prepared you, and now you are ready to step into greatness.

Edwin Louis Cole, in his book *Winners Are Not Those Who Never Fail, but Those Who Never Quit,* makes a profound statement, "We think in terms of avoiding crises, problems, punishment, correction and the hard issues of life because we are basically negative by nature. God's viewpoint is totally different. Because He is positive, God always thinks of releasing us to something, a better place or condition. In that sense, crisis is not as negative as the world or our perceptions would have us to believe. Transition is necessary for God to take you out of where we've been and into a better place."[3]

No one can live in this life without crisis. Both change and crisis are normal parts of life. Crisis is the natural result of change. The greater the degree of change, the greater the crisis. In fact, crisis is normal in the process of growth. We leave the old and enter the new by way of crisis.

What to Do When You Face a Crisis

When you face a crisis, trial, or setback in life you have three choices:

Choice 1—Do Absolutely Nothing

Choice 1 is not an option for a true leader. Why? Because your Bible says that your faith without works is dead (see James 2:26). Without corresponding actions to what you believe, you are not walking by faith. The Bible says that the "just" will *live* by faith. Therefore, faith is a way of life. To sit and do nothing is operating in fear. Leaders are courageous and move forward in the face to fear.

Choice 2—Give Up or Quit

Giving up and quitting are also not options for a true leader. Why? Because God did not design you to quit. He designed you to conquer and win in life! In order to conquer something, you must have opposition; without opposition you cannot have an enemy; and without an enemy you cannot have victory.

The crisis we face both individually and corporately can lead us to a better life, or become degenerative. The outcome rests not in the nature of the issue but in what we do with the crisis. The agony of failure and tormenting thoughts of giving up are feelings shared by "winners" and "losers" alike. What people do with the situation is what separates the winners from the losers. Winners are not those who never fail, but those who never quit.

—Edwin Louis Cole[4]

Choice 3—Believe God for Supernatural Promotion

Choice 3 is your only true option—believe God for supernatural promotion. True leaders are inspired by words such as: impossible, can't, hard, and challenging. You will never find a breakthrough in a "can't." Your miracle will be found in a "can."

> **_I can_** *do all things through Christ Jesus*
> *who strengthens me.*
>
> *Philippians 4:13*

Get Back Up!

People love comeback stories. That is why the movie *Rocky* and its sequels were so popular. People love to cheer for the underdog to win. You may be feeling a lot like Rocky Balboa. You have taken some serious and deadly hits. You are tired and at the end of your rope. You are down on the mat for the count. The referee is counting 1, 2, 3, 4, 5, 6, 7, 8, 9… Your situation looks grim. But WAIT! I have some good news for you! You have one more Holy Ghost punch in you. Get back up off the mat and give your adversary one more punch. The devil is the one who is going to go down for the count! I read the back of the Book, and you win! God has your comeback already scheduled.

Life was sweet when Michael J. Coles and a partner launched the Original Great American Chocolate Chip Cookie Company with $8,000. In the first month, his company pulled in $32,000. Then it happened. "I was on my way home on my motorcycle," recalls Coles. "I hit a rock and slammed into a telephone pole." He awoke the next morning in the hospital, with three limbs in casts and his face wrapped in bandages, but he slowly set about repairing his body and his business. Coles made what others thought was acceptable progress.

One day, he was hobbling up his driveway when his daughter challenged him to a race. He tried to run, and then he froze. "I realized I was mentally handicapped, too." Stung by humiliation, Coles took his first real step forward: "I decided that moment that whatever it took I would try to fully recover." He designed an excruciating rehabilitation program of weight lifting, squatting, and bicycling. "I set an impossible goal: I would become the best bicyclist around."

After four years of training, he bicycled across the country in 15½ days—a new world record. But all Coles could think about was breaking his own record. He did, two years later. Coles also pushed an aggressive franchise plan that has now reached sales of $70 million. "The accident taught me something," Coles muses. *"If you get run off the road, you get right up and start over again."*[5]

Refuse to accept defeat. Stop whining and complaining about the crisis, trial, or setback. Troubles are a lot like babies, they grow larger if you nurse them. Stop waiting for your ship to come in, and start swimming toward it. Life is like riding a bicycle, as long as you keep pedaling, you will not fall down.

People with Purpose

The transformation process can be better understood when you examine Ecclesiastics 3:1,*"To everything there is a season, A time for every purpose under heaven."* My first question for you: "Are you an *everything?*" Your answer should be yes. My next question: "Is a season an everything?" Your answer should again be yes. Based on those two answers, you can conclude three important facts about your life:

Fact 1—You were born for a reason and for a purpose.

Everything God created under Heaven, He created for a purpose. A cockroach is under Heaven. Therefore, a cockroach even has a purpose. I puzzle crowds when I make this statement. What is the purpose of a cockroach? The cockroach solves a problem. The purpose of a cockroach is to give the Orkin man a job. If God gave a cockroach an assignment on earth to fulfill, then you who were created in God's image must have a higher call and a greater purpose in life. There is

On December 29, 1987, a Soviet cosmonaut returned to the earth after 326 days in orbit. He was in good health, which hadn't always been the case in those record-breaking voyages. Five years earlier, touching down after 211 days in space, two cosmonauts suffered from dizziness, high pulse rates, and heart palpitations. They couldn't walk for a week, and after 30 days, they were still undergoing therapy for atrophied muscles and weakened hearts. At zero gravity, the muscles of the body begin to waste away because there is no resistance. To counteract this, the Soviets prescribed a vigorous exercise program for the cosmonauts. They invented the "penguin suit," a running suit laced with elastic bands. It resists every move the cosmonauts make, forcing them to exert their strength. Apparently the regimen is working.[7]

Many times we dream about days without struggle, resistance, or difficulty. God truly knows better. The easier our life, the weaker our spiritual fortitude. Character, spiritual growth, and strength of any kind only grows through resistance and exertion. A crisis is nothing more than an exercise machine used to build your faith muscles. This is the purpose of the valley season. God is building a vessel of honor. He is preparing you for the day when He will show you off to the world!

You may be crying out to God saying, "Lord, when are You going to change my situation; when am I going to see my breakthrough, when will I receive my miracle? God why are You allowing me to go through all of this?"

Here is your answer: *God is more concerned about changing you than He is about changing the circumstances around you.* If God can get what is inside you to change, then He will change your outside conditions. In a crisis, most people usually want God to do a *removing* job when He really wants to do an *improving* job.

Embrace the changes that God wants to do in your life. You are being prepared in the classroom of crisis for supernatural promotion.

ENDNOTES_____

1. Mark Chironna, Stepping into Greatness, (Lake Mary, FL: Creation House, 1999)

2. As quoted in Bob Phillips, Phillips' Book of Great Thoughts & Funny Sayings, (Wheaton, IL: Tyndale House Publishers, Inc, 1993), 81.

3. Edwin Louis Cole, *Winners Are Not Those Who Never Fail, but Those Who Never Quit* (Tulsa, OK: Albury Publishing, 1995).

4. Ibid.

5. *Success Magazine,* (July/August, 1989), 44.

6. Dr. Martin Luther King Jr., *The Strength to Love* (New York: Harper & Row, 1963), 20.

7. Craig Brian Larson, "My Daily Dose," Internet daily devotional.

CHAPTER TWO

TROUBLE: THE ROAD SIGN POINTING TOWARD PROMOTION

The story of the life of Moses is one of the greatest examples of a man who was being prepared to lead in crisis times. He faced a crisis, went through the process of change, and then experienced supernatural promotion. Moses was destined to lead the millions. Yet when Moses was 40 years old, in a fit of rage and anger, he killed an Egyptian man. Then he found himself on the backside of a mountain leading only a handful of dirty sheep for 40 years. Moses needed time of development and preparation before he would step into his full potential.

Forty is the number of testing, trial, probation, and a time of preparation. During the flood, in the days of Noah, it rained on earth for 40 days. What a time of preparation. You are in a season of preparation when you have to spend 40 days on a boat with your mother-in-law! Jesus even had to go through a season of preparation and crisis when He was led by the Holy Spirit into the wilderness for 40 days. During this time, it is reasonable to assume that Jesus was preparing Himself for the work the Father sent Him to do.

During this 40-year training period, God was preparing Moses. Then God appeared to him in a burning bush and says, *"Now therefore, behold, the cry of the children of Israel has come to Me, and I have also seen the oppression with which the Egyptians oppress them. Come now, therefore, and I will send you to Pharaoh that you may bring My people, the children of Israel, out of Egypt"* (Exodus 3:9-10).

Moses responds like many of us would respond, *"...O my Lord, I am not eloquent, neither before nor since You have spoken to Your servant; but I am slow of speech and slow of tongue"* (Exodus 4:10). Moses continues to tell God about all his limitations, while God is speaking to the potential of his destiny. God has more confidence in you, than you have in yourself. Convinced that he was unable to communicate, the Lord assigns Aaron to help Moses. The funny thing about this story is that as you read your Bible you find that Moses does most of the speaking. What Moses did not realize about himself is that God is preparing him for greatness on the backside of the mountain. Moses went through the process, now He is ready for promotion.

When you close your eyes to tragedy, you close your eyes to greatness.

—Stephen Vizinczey[1]

Watch Moses as he marches into Pharaoh's court, squares his back like a T-rail, puts his foot down, and points his finger in the face of his adversary and boldly says, "LET MY PEOPLE GO!" God built this man on the backside of the mountain— now the process was over and it was time for Moses to step into greatness! Moses became a hero and supernaturally led the children of Israel out of Egypt.

The children of Israel, just like Moses, had to go through the same process and preparation season. God purposely put Israel in an impossible situation on the other side of the Red Sea. The place where they stood is known in Hebrew as "the entrance to a precipitous cliff." The name also means "on the edge of crisis." God's people were getting ready to move into a season of preparation and testing before they entered into the Promised Land. They spent 40 years in the wilderness. Again, 40 is the number of preparation.

Preparing for Greatness

The Holy Spirit says to you and to me that we are in a season of preparation. He is preparing us and getting us ready for the greatest days of our lives. Everything you have been through up until today has been preparation for tomorrow.

The desire to win, be successful, or to do something great for God is not enough. The *will* to prepare to win is the most important thing. Champions are not just born. Champions are made in the process of preparation. Long before the Olympic gold medalists cross the finish line, they have spent countless hours, days, weeks, and months preparing themselves to win. The preparation time has brought a change in their muscle structure, their level of confidence, their character and their way of thinking. Winners pay the price of preparation. The price to pay is the currency of time.

Champions do not become champions in the ring. They are merely recognized in the ring. Their becoming happens in their daily routine.

—Source Unknown

Preparation is the difference between winning and losing. You are already preparing, whether you know it or not. The question: what are you preparing for? To win or to just finish? Success or failure? H.P. Liddon said, "What we do on some great occasion will probably depend on what we already are. And what we are will be the result of previous years of self-discipline." What you are doing today is preparing you for your tomorrow. When you learn to do the right things every day, you are guaranteed success in your tomorrow. If you continue to do the wrong things today, you are guaranteed failure in your future.

Before anything else, getting ready is the secret of success.

—Henry Ford

The Bible focuses more on the process than on the "big event." You are in a process (whether you resist it or not) of becoming the person God meant you to be. Without a desire to prepare and improve yourself, growth is impossible.

Do you want to experience promotion? Do you long to step into greatness? Do you want your career, ministry, or business to take off? If your answer is yes, then what are you doing today to prepare you for tomorrow? What books are you reading? What classes are you taking? What are you doing to develop your skills, knowledge, and talents? Are you listening to audio tapes from your mentor or from somebody who knows more than you about your field of interest? Are you practicing every day to win?

When you are not practicing, remember someone, somewhere, is practicing; and when you meet him, he will win.

—Bill Bradley

Joshua was 40 years old when he was sent with the twelve to spy out the Promised Land. This man had faithfully served Moses. His mind was renewed and he had great faith in what God could do. Joshua was prepared and ready to step into supernatural promotion. How do I know this? Because after 40 days of spying out the Promised Land, Joshua came back with a positive report saying:

"The land we passed through to spy out is an exceedingly good land. If the LORD delights in us, then He will bring us into this land and give it to us, 'a land which flows with milk and honey.' Only do not rebel against the LORD, nor fear the people of the land, for they are our bread; their protection has departed from them, and the LORD is with us. Do not fear them" (Numbers 14:7-9).

Unfortunately, the other ten spies were not prepared and came back with a negative report. The children of Israel listened to the negative report and found themselves taking another lap around the mountain. They obviously needed more preparation time. They had physically left Egypt, but they had not mentally left Egypt.

Crisis—Process—Crisis—Process—Crisis

What can we learn from this story? It is possible for you to face a crisis that moves you into process, and in the process you refuse to change or you just simply do not prepare yourself to change. Therefore, you end up in a viscous cycle of going from crisis to process, to crisis to process, to crisis to process, and eventually you die never stepping into greatness. Graveyards are full of people who never stepped into their full potential. Why? Because they refused to change, learn, and grow in the process. All things are possible, as long as you do not die in the wilderness or crisis season. Do you see the importance of refusing to remain who you are? You must embrace change in the process! Your life depends on it.

Joseph faced a crisis when his brothers threw him in the pit after he shared his dream that one day he would be ruling and reigning and his brothers would come and bow down to him. The beginning of a dream often generates more enthusiasm than wisdom. Joseph had to learn some things before he would step into his destiny.

The first principle that Joseph had to learn: Do not try to share an 8 by 12 vision with 3 by 5 minds. Joseph's brothers were jealous of his dream. This landed Joseph in the pit. I believe that it was in the pit where Joseph learned this very important principle: Even a fish would not get caught if it kept its mouth shut. How many times have you made this same mistake?

Joseph's promise was the palace, but he found himself in the pit and the prison. Just think about what God can do for you in one day? One morning Joseph was in the prison. He woke up on a hard and dirty bed, eating stale bread, drinking lukewarm water, and wearing prisoner clothes. However, when Joseph went to bed that night he was wearing an Armani suit, eating filet mignon and lobster tail, and sleeping on a bed of ivory with satin sheets (Keith Johnson Translation). In one day, Joseph went from rags to riches, from being a prisoner to being the vice president of an entire country.

Sometimes you have to go through the "P's" in life to get to the "P's." You have to go through the pit, prison, problem, persecution, pain, people, peril, perplexity, and poverty, to get to the palace, purpose, promise, prosperity, peace, provision, and promotion. After all the troubles Joseph faced, in the last chapter of Genesis he was able to boldly say, *"But as for you, you meant evil against me; but God meant it for good, in order to bring it about as it is this day, to save many people alive* (Genesis 50:20).

Job knew what it is like to face a major crisis. He was a righteous man who loved and feared God. Yet, He faced the loss of all his children due to death. He faced financial ruin. Job also faced a demonic assault of sickness in his physical body. Many Bible scholars say that this season lasted for six months. Job was being tested in the process (see Job 23:10). Finally, Job's breakthrough came and the Bible states that the Lord returned double for His trouble:

*And the LORD restored Job's losses when he prayed for his friends. Indeed the LORD gave Job **twice** as much as he had before. Now the LORD blessed the latter days of Job more than his beginning; for he had fourteen thousand sheep, six thousand camels, one thousand yoke of oxen, and one thousand female donkeys* (Job 42:10,12).

We see in the trial of Job, the marvelous grace of God that brings blessings out of being broken, celebration out of calamity, prosperity out of poverty, health out of sickness, and triumph out of tragedy. What God did for Job, He can and will do for you. God will compensate you for the loses that occurred during a crisis. You can declare double for all your personal mistakes and you can decree a sevenfold return of all that the devil has stolen from you (see Proverbs 6:30-31).

The Making of a Great Leader:
Crisis—Process—Promotion

A crisis is nothing more than a launching pad to success, a doorway to promotion. Every great leader had to face difficult and trying times. The reason they are called great is because they did not quit. Their persistence wore out their resistance and they won the victory. Your crisis is a bridge, not a roadblock, to making you a more effective leader. *You will learn more in the classroom of crisis than you will ever learn in the place of comfort and ease.*

Many of God's chosen leaders throughout the Bible continually experienced one crisis after another. Daniel faced a crisis when he was thrown into the lions' den. God sent an angel to shut the lions' mouths. The next day the king found Daniel alive and unharmed and then promoted Daniel to second in command.

Refusing to compromise their faith in God, Shadrack, Meshach, and Abednego were thrown into a fiery furnace. They discovered that there was a fourth man in the furnace. When you walk through the fires and storms of life, God will be with you. After the crisis, these three men were supernaturally promoted by King Nebuchadnezzar.

Esther and her uncle Mordecai faced a crisis when Haman set a decree to kill all the Jews in the land. For three days they fasted and prayed. Esther found favor in the sight of King Ahasuerus. Instead of the king killing the Jewish people, Haman was hanged on the gallows. Then Esther and Mordecai were promoted by the king.

Jesus Christ himself faced a crisis when he went to the cross. For three days He was in Hell. Then on the third day, as the devil watched, Jesus Christ resurrected from the dead and showed Himself to many. The Lord then instructed His disciples for the next 40 days after His resurrection.

The disciples faced a major setback when they lost their Leader. They had followed Jesus for three and a half years. Only John is to be found at the cross. Peter and the boys were in a process of change. Nevertheless, Peter stepped into greatness after he received the power of the Holy Spirit. He stood up and preached the first great gospel message and 3,000 souls came into the Kingdom in one day.

The apostle Paul was destined to preach the gospel to royalty. Yet look what the apostle Paul went through in his effort to obey the will of God for his life:

*Are they ministers of Christ?—I speak as a fool—I am more: in labors more abundant, in stripes above measure, **in prisons** more frequently, **in deaths often**. From the Jews **five times** I received **forty stripes** minus one. **Three times** I was **beaten with rods**; **once** I was stoned; **three times** I was **shipwrecked**; a night and a day I have been in the deep; in journeys often, in perils of waters, in perils of robbers, in perils of my own countrymen, in perils of the Gentiles, in perils in the city, in perils in the wilderness, in perils in the sea, in perils among false brethren; in weariness and toil, in sleeplessness often, **in hunger and thirst**, in fastings often, **in cold and nakedness;** besides the other things, what comes upon me daily: my deep concern for all the churches.*

—2 Corinthians 11:23-28
(Emphasis Added)

After it all, one day apostle Paul stepped into greatness and stood before King Agrippa. Paul preached such an effective sermon that a totally ungodly king says, *"You almost persuade me to become a Christian"* (Acts 26:28).

For a great and effective door has opened to me, and there are many adversaries.

—Apostle Paul

Long before you get to your doorway of promise, you have to walk down the hallway of adversity. The hallway to your destiny will be filled with D's: Demons, Distractions, Discouragements, and Disappointments. Your turnaround is just ahead, you have come too far to go back now. Just keep walking down the hall—you can be an overcomer, a leader through times of crisis.

Concluding Thoughts

Pretend that you are a third party looking into all of the crisis situations. As you observe Daniel in the lions' den, Joseph in prison, Job's life falling apart, the widow's last meal, the three Hebrew boys being thrown into the furnace, and a Man who never committed sin hanging naked on an old rugged cross, you would have to say, "That looks wrong, God! Why?" Here is a powerful principle to place into your spirit: *What looks wrong is sometimes right, and what looks right is sometimes wrong—because God sees beyond the crisis.*

God looks beyond the crisis and sees the promotion that was waiting just ahead of these biblical leaders. He does the same for you. Walking daily with the Holy Spirit is the only way to discern the decisions you need to make in life about your future.

This is why you also need a mentor in your life. When you find your mentor, you have found a true miracle in life. Why? Because the person has walked through everything that you are getting ready to walk through. He (or she if you are a woman) has made wrong decisions when everything looked right. He has turned things down that looked wrong, only to find out that it was right all the time. Your mentor can warn and advise you of detours and distractions. Gaining wisdom by mistakes and failures is not the best way to learn. Obtaining wisdom and knowledge from a spiritual mentor will save you a lot of future heartache.

You must recognize your mentor when God brings one into your life. Elisha recognized Elijah. Joshua recognized Moses. Ruth recognized Naomi. The disciples recognized Jesus. Timothy recognized Paul. Many successful people will tell you that they would not have achieved their current level of success if a mentor or teacher had not been in their life. Who has God placed in your life to mentor and help you?

Crisis—a Road Sign that Promotion Is Near!

Your crisis is actually a road sign that promotion is on the way. Why? Because crisis always precedes supernatural promotion. The very fact that you have trouble is proof that promotion is on the way. If you are facing a financial crisis, guess what? A financial breakthrough is on the way! Are you sick? Then get ready because God's healing power is about to penetrate your body. Are your children acting up and not serving the Lord? Then get ready for a spiritual awakening in your family.

When written in Chinese the word crisis is composed of two characters. One represents danger and the other represents opportunity.

—John F. Kennedy

I always tried to turn every disaster into an opportunity.

—John D. Rockefeller

Men and Women Who Refused to Quit

There have been men and women throughout history who have faced tremendous tragedies and setbacks. These are people who have used their crisis to make them a stronger and a better person. They are people who have learned to turn their trouble into triumph and their setbacks into stepping stones. Let's look at a few of these people in our modern times.

Johnny Fulton was run over by a car at the age of three. He suffered crushed hips, broken ribs, a fractured skull, and compound fractures in his legs. It did not look as if he would live. But he would not give up. In fact, later in life ran the half-mile in less than two minutes.

Walt Davis was totally paralyzed by polio when he was nine years old, but he did not give up. He became the Olympic high jump champion in 1952.

Shelly Mann was paralyzed by polio when she was five years old, but she would not give up. She eventually claimed eight different swimming records for the U.S. and won a gold medal at the 1956 Olympics in Melbourne, Australia.

In 1938, Karoly Takacs, a member of Hungary's world-champion pistol shooting team and sergeant in the army, lost his right hand when a grenade he was holding exploded. But Takacs did not give up. He learned to shoot left-handed and won gold medals in the 1948 and 1952 Olympics.

Lou Gehrig was such a clumsy ball player that the boys in his neighborhood would not let him play on their team. But he was committed. He did not give up. Eventually, his name was entered into baseball's Hall of Fame.

Woodrow Wilson could not read until he was ten years old, but he was a committed person. He became the twenty-eighth President of the United States.

During the greater part of his life, American historian Francis Parkman suffered so acutely that he could not work for more than five minutes at a time. His eyesight was so wretched that he could scrawl only a few gigantic words on a manuscript, yet he contrived to write twenty magnificent volumes of history.[2]

Ludwig van Beethoven went deaf. From his seventh symphony on, this man wrote without the physical ability to hear.

Raised in abject poverty, Abraham Lincoln overcame his humble beginnings by reading everything he could find, and he rose through the ranks to become one of America's greatest presidents. If he would have succumbed to the failure of losing many elections before running for the presidency, Lincoln would have stayed a country lawyer, just working to make ends meet.

Glen Cunningham was told by the doctors that he would never walk again, but he went on to run the mile and break the world record in 1934.

Albert Einstein was diagnosed with Asberger Syndrome. They said Einstein would never learn, go to school, ride a bike, or play with other children because he was unreachable and retarded.

Wayne Gretzky, unarguably the greatest hockey player that ever set foot on a rink, was told when he tried out for the pros that he was fifty pounds too light. But he refused to quit.

Michael Jordan, unarguably the greatest basketball player to ever set foot on a court, was cut by the coach from his high school basketball team. But he refused to quit.

Dr. Seuss submitted his first book, *And to Think I Saw It on Mulberry Street*, to twenty-six publishers, with twenty-six rejections for his effort. But the twenty-seventh publisher accepted it, and the rest is literature history.[3]

Terry Fox, a young Canadian completed the greatest marathon run in history. He averaged a marathon a day for five months. Running a total of 3,339 miles across Canada. The truly remarkable thing is that Terry Fox is an amputee.[4]

Those who have experienced the thrills of victories and accomplishments have all passed through the storms of life. There are three essential truths that you must grasp during your time of crisis:

Truth 1—God thinks seasonally.

God does not have a wrist watch. God is eternal. He is not bound by time. To understand the processes of God, you must understand how God thinks. When God created the earth, He was thinking of seasons. That is why there is a spring, summer, fall, and winter. Each season brings a dynamic of change. Seasons are God's natural way of leading you from one dimension to another. These seasons can not be stopped and they better not be ignored. One who acts in winter as though it is summer could die. One who ignores the planting season will be waiting a very long time for a future harvest.

Truth 2—God is in control of every season.

*And He [God] **changes** the times and the seasons; He removes kings and raises up kings; He gives wisdom to the wise and knowledge to those who have understanding.*

—Daniel 2:21, see also Acts 1:7
(Emphasis Added)

The good news is that seasons are temporary. Every season has a beginning and an end. Your season of sickness, lack, or struggle will not last forever. The seasons of your life will have different time lengths as well. Some seasons will be long and others will be short. Keep your eyes on the Lord, He is the only One who can bring change to your present season.

Truth 3—God is with you in the crisis or valley season.

*But Zion said, "The LORD has forsaken me, and my Lord has forgotten me." "Can a woman forget her nursing child, and not have compassion on the son of her womb? Surely they may forget, yet I will not forget you. See, **I have inscribed you on the palms of My hands;** your walls are continually before Me."*

Isaiah 49:14-16
(Emphasis Added)

No matter what you are going through, God has not forgotten you! The Amplified version of Isaiah 49:16 says that God has you tattooed a picture of you in the palm of His hands.

All around the world there are people who should be sitting in our church services but are not because they have given up on God. Why? Because they did not understand the valley seasons. When trouble or tragedy came, thousands turned their back on God. Many have said, "If God loves me and cares about me, then why am I going though all of this? What is the use in serving God? Every time I do, bad things seem to start happening to me." The enemy has lied to many people, convincing them that God does not care and that He is not real.

If you are facing a crisis, don't be deceived. Do not give up now. Your turnaround and promotion is on the way!

ENDNOTES

1. *A Biography*, in *Sunday Telegraph* (London, 5 Jan. 1984; repr. in *Truth and Lies in Literature,* 1986).

2. Tim Hansel, *You Gotta Keep Dancin'* (Ontario, Canada: David C. Cook), 566.

3. Rod Parsley, *The Day Before Eternity* (Lake Mary, FL: Creation House 1998), 42-43.

4. David McNally, *Even Eagles Need a Push* (New York: Dell Publishing 1990), 31.

CHAPTER THREE

STEPPING INTO GREATNESS

People today are willing to settle for so little in life. Many people like to camp out in the valley. Why? Because it is a comfortable or a familiar place. You have to get out of your "comfort zone" to go to a higher level in life. God has not destined you as a leader to live in the valley with all the other chickens. You were created to soar like an eagle high above the highest mountain peaks. You will never know your full potential until you boldly step out of your comfort zone. Change must take place in the valley season before you will experience supernatural promotion. During your crisis season, you may think that you are waiting on God to bring you a breakthrough. When in fact, you are not waiting on God, but God is waiting on you to change.

As an eagle stirs up its nest, hovers over its young, spreading out its wings, taking them up, carrying them on its wings, so the LORD alone led him, and there was no foreign god with him.

Deuteronomy 32:11-12

This Scripture in Deuteronomy is a wonderful picture from the Word of God that teaches us about the processes of God. Before the eaglets are born, the mother eagle lines the bottom of the nest with her feathers. This gives the eaglets a nice soft place to lay and sleep. During the development stages of a baby eaglet, the mother takes care of her babies. When the baby eaglets mature and they are ready to leave the nest and fly, the mother eagle bristly flaps her wings over the nest to get the cushion of the feathers out of the bottom of the nest. This causes the eaglets to become uncomfortable. As long as they remain in the nest, they will never enter into their full potential. The twigs, thorns, and bark begin to prick the eaglets—they face a crisis. Dissatisfaction causes them to move out of the nest. Now the mother can teach her babies how to fly. After a process of several attempts to fly, the eaglets will finally step into greatness and fly like the mature and magnificent eagles they will become.

Circumstances and crises are God's tools to move you into your purpose and the maximizing of your potential.

—Dr. Myles Munroe

Just as the eagle stirs her nest to get the eaglets to move into their full potential, so the Lord will allow you to go through a season of discomfort, so that you will move into a process of change. Security, satisfaction, and comfort are your enemies to living at your full potential. Seasons of divine dissatisfaction and divine provoking is the Lord's way of getting you out of your comfort zone. Then you, like the eaglet, will move out of your comfort zone and soar into your full potential.

While the mother eagle was stirring up the nest, I'm sure the first thought of the eaglet was, *Why are you doing this*

Mom? During a crisis season people always ask, "Why?" The children of Israel were no doubt asking that same question as they journeyed through the wilderness for 40 years.

Deuteronomy 8 gives the answer to all our questions concerning the purpose of difficult times in our lives:

> *And you shall remember that the LORD your God led you all the way these forty years in the wilderness, **to humble you** and **test you**, to know what was in your heart, whether you would keep His commandments or not. So He humbled you, allowed you to hunger, and fed you with manna which you did not know nor did your fathers know, that He might **make you know** that man shall not live by bread alone; but man lives by every word that proceeds from the mouth of the LORD.*
>
> *Deuteronomy 8:2-3*
> (Emphasis Added)

God allowed Israel to go through the wilderness or crisis season for four purposes: to humble them, to test them, to teach them, and to promote them.

Why the Crisis? To Humble You!

"...To humble you...."

—GOD
(Deuteronomy 8:2)

A young seminary graduate came up to the lectern, very self-confident and immaculately dressed. He began to deliver his first sermon in his first church and the words simply would not come out. Finally he burst into tears and ended up leaving the platform obviously humbled. There were two older ladies sitting in the front row and one remarked to the other, "If he'd come in like he went out, he would have gone out like he came in."[1]

The hardest lesson for human beings to learn in this world is the lesson of humility. This lesson is not taught in secular schools, seminaries, and at most Bible colleges. You will only learn this lesson in the classroom of crisis. Jesus taught His disciples to live in humility when He says, *"...learn from Me, for I am gentle and lowly in heart, and you will find rest for your souls* (Matthew 11:29). Teaching the disciples true humility was Jesus' toughest assignment.

> ## Pride, like cocaine, deceives its victims into over-confidence.
>
> —*Mario Murrillo*

Humility is not thinking and acting like a worm in the dirt. Humility is not thinking less of yourself. Humility is thinking less about yourself. It is simply maintaining an utter dependency upon God. Without His help, guidance, and protection we are finished (see John 15:5). We need His presence, anointing, and divine direction every day of our lives. Look what happens when you become prideful and start depending on your self, talents, accomplishments, and education:

> ## It thrust proud Nebuchadnezzar out of men's society, proud Saul out of his kingdom, proud Adam out of paradise, proud Haman out of court, proud Lucifer out of heaven.
>
> —*Henry Smith*

It takes true humility to admit that you are wrong. Pride will keep you in a state of denial. The enemy to lasting change is to pretend like everything is OK when it's not. Pride says, "I do not need to change! Nothing is wrong with me, I'm fine. This is just the way I am, and if you do not like me, that's tough." Refusing to admit that you need to change prevents you from moving into your full potential.

Humble pie may taste awful, but it contains much nourishment.

—Croft M. Pentz

It also takes humility to admit personal failures in the past. The greatest communicators in the world are those who are willing to share their shattered lives, failures, limitations, and setbacks—and then can communicate the lessons they learned in their crisis and how they overcame their troubles.

For those who would learn God's ways, humility is the first thing, humility is the second, humility is the third. —Saint Augustine

Many people are prideful in what they believe. You can build walls around error that change will have no access to. Pride will keep you from asking questions, because you are afraid of appearing stupid. The humble person is teachable and will listen to new information.

The valley season teaches you to be more dependent on God. You learn to stop depending on yourself. You cannot make it on your own. It takes humility to admit that you need help. The crisis season teaches you to allow God and others to help you fulfill your assignment in life.

The crisis season has a way of conquering our pride. Pride is truly the greatest enemy to change. Pride keeps you in your comfort zone. Humility moves you toward the promotion zone. Here are five road signs that reveal pride in your life:

Road Sign 1—Strife: arguing, fighting, etc.

*By pride comes nothing but strife, but
with the well-advised is wisdom.*

—*Proverbs 13:10*

Road Sign 2—Destruction

*Pride goes before destruction, and a
haughty spirit before a fall.*

—*Proverbs 16:18*

Road Sign 3—Captivity

*Hear and give ear: Do not be proud, for the LORD
has spoken. Give glory to the LORD your God
before He causes darkness…But if you will not
hear it, my soul will weep in secret for **your pride**;
my eyes will weep bitterly and run down with tears,
because the Lord's flock has been **taken captive**.*

—*Jeremiah 13:15-17*
(Emphasis Added)

Road Sign 4—Shame, embarrassment, and guilt

*When pride comes, then comes shame;
but with the humble is wisdom.*

—*Proverbs 11:2*

*For whoever exalts himself will be humbled, and
he who humbles himself will be exalted.*

—*Luke 14:11*

Road Sign 5—Lack of respect

*A man's pride will bring him low, but the humble in spirit will retain **honor.***

—*Proverbs 29:23*
(Emphasis Added)

Many people will never change until the pain of where they are is so great that they have no option but to change. The pain and pressure of your crisis should cause you to pray, *"Search me, O God, and know my heart; try me, and know my anxieties; and see if there is any wicked way in me, and lead me in the way everlasting* (Psalm 139:23-24). God's grace is free, but there is one essential requirement to receiving it—humility. *"But He gives more grace. Therefore He says: 'God resists the proud, but gives grace to the humble'"* (James 4:6).

When you refuse to walk in humility, you close the door to God's divine direction in your life. *"The humble **He guides** in justice, and the humble **He teaches** His way"* (Psalm 25:9).

Why the Crisis? To Test You!

"...and test you..."

—*GOD*
(Deuteronomy 8:2)

A car coming off the assembly line is tested before it is sold at a dealership. Cooks test their sauces before they serve it to the customers. A computer programmer tests new programs before they are sold to a manufacturer. The only way for a teacher to know if students have learned their lessons is by giving them an examination. The test exposes the level of maturity and knowledge of the students. Every new product is tested before it is released to the public for use. God permits testings for the purpose of building faith, strength, and character in a person.

*I, the LORD, search the heart, I **test** the mind, even to give every man according to his ways, according to the fruit of his doings.*

—*Jeremiah 17:10*
(Emphasis Added)

*...For the righteous God **tests** the hearts and minds.*

—*Psalm 7:9*
(Emphasis Added)

When God tests a person He always provides a way of escape (see 1 Cor. 10:13). God does not test you with the intent that you will fail, but that you will succeed. God does not test you with evil but with good. Satan tempts people with evil or sin for the purpose of destruction. God does not tempt you, but the Lord will test you, His prime possession, to see if you are ready to go to the next level. These are not pencil and paper exams but life experience tests. The testing comes in the seasons of "Nothing seems to be happening," and "Everything seems to be falling apart."

The Lord takes His time in developing you. He is more concerned about building people rather than building large businesses and churches. God wants to put His qualities inside you before He puts His name on the product when it goes out. God wants to make sure the foundation is in place before He builds a great skyscraper.

God grooms us for greatness in the stockades of struggle.

—*Bishop T.D. Jakes*

What is God testing during a crisis? He is testing your faith, strength, and character; *"Knowing that the testing of your faith produces patience. But let patience have its perfect work, that you may be perfect and complete, lacking nothing"* (James 1:3-4). Why does God allow you to be tested? God is preparing you to make you perfect and complete. If you do not pass the test, God will not allow you to drop out of His school. The Lord will make you take the test until you pass. Therefore, don't wait for a crisis to determine if your faith is strong!

God tested Abraham, *"By faith Abraham, when he was **tested,** offered up Isaac, and he who had received the promises offered up his only begotten son* (Hebrews 11:17). The people who pass the test are those who have learned to obey the voice of the Holy Spirit. The Word of God even instructs us to test people before we put them into leadership positions, *"But let these also first be **tested**; then let them serve as deacons, being found blameless"* (1 Timothy 3:10). I tell pastors all the time, "The best way to test those who want to work in your ministry is to give them cleaning utensils and tell them to start cleaning the toilets. You will find out real quick whether you have a servant of the Lord or a playboy. A team player or a person looking to be a superstar."

Why the Crisis? To Teach You!

"That He might make you know that man shall not live by bread alone; but man lives by every word that proceeds from the mouth of the LORD."

—GOD
(Deuteronomy 8:3)

I like to walk in the morning. I usually walk by myself, but there are days I will walk with my wife or a friend. Whenever

I walk with someone, I talk to them along the way. It would be very rude of me to go on a five-mile walk and never say a word to the person I am walking with. Enoch walked with God. Noah walked with God. In the Garden of Eden, Adam walked daily with God.

God is not rude. When you walk daily with Him, He will talk to you. When God speaks to you, He will often say at least one or four things:

1. He gives you a promise.

The Lord will give you a promise about your future. The promise will energize you and give you faith to step out of your comfort zone and launch into your future. Faith comes by hearing both the written (Logos) Word of God and the spoken (rhema) Word of God. *"So then faith comes by hearing, and hearing by the Word* [rhema] *of God"* (Romans 10:17). The rhema word is what God is saying today. According to W.E. Vines, the Greek word *rhema* is "not the whole Bible, but a specific word given by God for a specific situation at a specific time." This would be a word that you feel "burning" in your heart.

2. He will give you instructions.

The Lord will also give you instructions. Every time the Lord sets out to bless you, He will give you an instruction. If you obey the instruction, you will experience supernatural promotion. Your last act of obedience then qualifies you for a new instruction. You will not receive instruction #2 until you obey instruction #1.

3. He gives you warnings and corrections.

The Lord will also warn you about different potholes in the road ahead of you on your journey of life. God warned Noah about a coming flood. He warned Joseph about the coming famine. The Lord warned Abraham about the destruction of Sodom and Gomorrah. The Holy Spirit warned Paul about the "chains" that awaited him in Jerusalem. Jesus warned the disciples and the Jewish people that both Jerusalem and the Temple would be destroyed. Forty years later this prophecy was fulfilled. God gave them 40 years to embrace the changes and step into greatness. These divine warnings help you prepare in advance for a coming crisis.

The Holy Spirit also brings correction. He speaks to you about issues of your conduct, marriage, obedience to the will of God for your life, negative confessions, your love walk, and in general about your personal life lining up with the Word of God.

4. He gives you affirmation.

Many times God will affirm to you that you are loved, accepted, forgiven, and valuable. He also lets you know that you are a son or daughter of God and that you are pleasing Him. Jesus Christ Himself needed these words of affirmation from God the Father (see Matthew 3:17).

God wants to teach you in the crisis season to daily walk with Him and listen to His voice. The instructions, promises, warnings, and affirmations the Lord gives you one day may not be the same the next day. Many people's prayer life consists of a lot of talking to God. Few people have learned the concept of being quiet and listening to the voice of the Holy Spirit. Please note: God gave humanity two ears and one mouth. Why? Because He wants you to listen twice as much as you talk.

Job learned the importance of listening to the word of the Lord during his crisis, *"But He knows the way that I take; when He has tested me, I shall come forth as gold. My foot has held fast to His steps; I have kept His way and not turned aside. I have not departed from the commandment of His lips; I have* **treasured** *the* **words of His mouth** *more than my necessary food"* (Job 23:10-12).

This is the principle that God wanted to teach the children of Israel in the desert:

> *__Hear,__ O My people, and I will admonish you! O Israel, if you will __listen__ to Me! There shall be no foreign god among you; nor shall you worship any foreign god. I am the LORD your God, Who brought you out of the land of Egypt; Open your mouth wide, and I will fill it. But My people __would not heed My voice,__ And Israel would have none of Me. So I gave them over to their own stubborn heart, to walk in their own counsels. Oh, that My people would __listen__ to Me, That Israel would walk in My ways! I would soon subdue their enemies, and turn My hand against their adversaries. The haters of the LORD would pretend submission to Him, but their fate would endure forever. He would have fed them also with the finest of wheat; And with honey from the rock I would have satisfied you.*
>
> *—Psalm 81:8-16*
> (Emphasis Added)

In the wilderness they were to follow the cloud by day and the fire by night. This required the Israelites to live in daily obedience. If they refused to move forward, they would find themselves in a crisis situation. They would have no clouds to shade them from the sun, and no fire to keep them warm at night.

It Is Time to Move Forward!

God demands forward movement. If your desire does not move you toward God, your crisis will. A crisis will force you to move. You will either move toward God or you will move away from God. Nonetheless, you will move. This is why Jesus says in Matthew 11:28, *"**Come** to Me, all you who labor and are heavy laden, and I will give you rest.* The apostle James told us to *"**Draw near** to God and He will draw near to you..."* (James 4:8). To "come" or to "draw near" demands forward movement from you as an individual.

Many people draw back when the pressures of life come against them. Henry Ford put a reverse gear in the model-T, but God never put a reverse gear in His people. We are supposed to be moving from faith to faith, from victory to victory, and from glory to glory. In Him we live and *move* and have our being—out of your belly shall *flow forth* rivers of living water.

A river is moving and is full of living things. Anything that is not moving becomes stagnate. A swamp has no intake and no outlet. Therefore, a swamp has no movement. The only things that like to live in swamps are snakes, crocodiles, and mosquitoes. The modern church today is full of snakes who have slithered their way into leadership positions in the church. We have a bunch of crocodiles in the church who love to back bite and tear leaders and people apart. The church is also crammed full of mosquitoes. What does a mosquito do? They suck blood out of living things, giving nothing back in return.

Success...seems to be connected with action. Successful people keep moving. They make mistakes, but they don't quit.

—Conrad Hilton

When you start sitting, you start rotting. Only dead things rot. Dead things do not desire change or improvement. Have you ever gone to a funeral and seen a dead person rise out of the coffin and say, "Can you comb my hair and change the clothes I am wearing?" Successful people live with this question, "How can I improve myself, business, ministry, or marriage? How can I do better?" When you stop desiring improvement you start rotting. When you start rotting you also start stinking.

The modern church today is full of people who only want to sit on their pews and they end up smelling like pew! They do nothing for the Kingdom of God, but expect the local church to pour into their lives by teaching them the Word, providing free marriage counseling, babysitting their children while they attend church, and give them a free hand-out when they are short of cash. And God forbid if the preacher ever talks about money or giving a special offering.

Somebody once said that man is made of dust and dust tends to settle. People tend to settle down and do the same things year in and year out, slowly going around in a circle. When this gets into religion, it is deadly and evil.

—A.W. Tozer

History has shown us that humans have a tendency to build monuments around past events. A monument is a stationary structure that man builds to reflect back to former victories, tragedies, or failures. The Church of Jesus Christ has a tendency to build monuments on former spiritual awakenings and former moves of God. Then we make a monument, called a denomination or fellowship, out of that particular movement. The question is not, "What did God say or do in 1904?" The real question is, "What is God saying and doing today?"

In the Old Testament, man *walked* with God. However, the New Testament believer is to *run* with God (see Hebrews 12:1). You cannot walk or run forward into your future as long as you remain chained to your past. Many people are chained to past moves of God, traditions, policies, hurts, failures, and wrong belief systems. It is time to start running forward. The cloud is moving. In the wilderness, God told the children of Israel, *You have been on this mountain long enough* (see Deuteronomy 1:6). It is time for you to let go of the past, so you can run into today's blessings.

Why the Crisis? To Promote You!

" ...to do you good in the end."

—*GOD*
(Deuteronomy 8:16)

Through 40 years of struggles, hardships, and failures, the Israelites finally entered into the Promised Land. It was time for God's people to experience supernatural promotion. This place of supernatural abundance was full of brooks, springs, wheat, barley, pomegranates, olive oil, honey, beautiful houses, herds, flocks, silver, and gold. The process and preparation season had paid off. This would be a place where God's chosen people would *"lack nothing"* (Deuteronomy 8:9).

Many people want to drive around the process and preparation season and instantly step into greatness. However, the greater the work you allow God to do in you, the greater the work God will do through you. The size of the struggle is an indicator of the size of the promotion. When there is a great struggle, there will also be a great promotion.

The apostle Peter had struggled all night trying to catch some fish, but he caught nothing. How would you like to work a twelve-hour day and not get paid for it? I define that as a crisis. How do you think Peter was feeling that morning? Like a failure? I think so. Then Jesus told Peter to launch his boat out into the deep and let down his nets for a catch. Although Peter was tired, He obeyed the "now" word of the Lord. Look what happened after he obeyed:

And when they had done this, they caught a great number of fish, and their net was breaking. So they signaled to their partners in the other boat to come and help them. And they came and filled both the boats, so that they began to sink.

—Luke 5:6-7

Peter faced the crisis of failure, which took him through the process of change. He then embraced the "now" Word of the Lord and stepped into supernatural promotion. He received such a large harvest that his nets broke and the boats started to sink. Peter's obedience caused him to receive an abundant supply. Now Peter could start blessing and helping other fishermen with the same problems around him.

The end result of your crisis season is to prepare you to help someone else when they go through the same crisis, *"And the One* [God] *who so wonderfully comforts and strengthens us in our hardships and trials. And why does He do this? So that when others are troubled, needing our sympathy and encouragement, we can pass on to them this same help and comfort God has given us"* (2 Corinthians 1:4 The Living Bible). God can use your personal "bad experience" to help another person. Your personal crisis will help you in the future give great council, comfort, and wisdom to others.

What you make happen for others, God will make happen for you.

—*Mike Murdock*

The theme concept of many multi-level marketing businesses is "make someone else a success, and they will make you a success." This is actually a Kingdom principle, *"knowing that whatever good anyone does, he will receive the same from the Lord..."* (Ephesians 6:8).

Take the time to help somebody else on their journey of life. You have the answer to somebody's problem. The solution to that problem can be the key that will unlock the door to supernatural promotion in your own life. The promotion may come from the business or ministry you start, the book you write, or the person you help.

God does not owe us an explanation for everything. Besides, explanations don't take away the pain. Even when we know why a tragedy happens, it still hurts. It is more helpful to ask "How" and "What." How can I grow from this situation, and what does God want me to learn from it?

—*Pastor Rick Warren*

Instead of asking God "Why the crisis?" take time to ask God, "What are the hurts or problems in peoples' lives that You are calling me to solve or deal with?"

ENDNOTES

1. Quick Verse for Windows, 1992-1996, Graig Rairdin and Parson Technology Inc., Bible Illustrator.

CHAPTER FOUR

WHAT TO DO WHEN EVERYTHING FALLS APART

John F. Kennedy Junior's plane crash was a terrible tragedy. Experts say that the crash was caused by the lack of instrument training John Jr. had. When flying in a storm, confusion can come when it is dark, cloudy, and foggy. During these times, it is important for a pilot to rely on the gages to successfully fly through the storm.

If a pilot uses his intuition to fly the plane in foggy or stormy weather, he may think he is right side up when in fact he may be upside down. One wrong move of the control stick and the result can be devastating. Possibly even causing the plane to crash and burn.

God has given you an instrument panel to keep you from crashing and burning in the midst of your storm or crisis. His instrument panel is called the Word of God—the Bible. When you are going through a storm you must keep your eyes on the Word of God. Storms are dangerous. The storms of life can sink you. I can classify every person's current state in one of three categories:

Category 1 - You have just gone through a storm.

Category 2 - You are in a storm right now.

Category 3 - You are getting ready to face a storm.

I know you would like to rebuke Category 3. Trust me, I have tried myself. But Jesus Christ told us that the storms of life will blow on the godly and the ungodly alike:

> *Therefore whoever hears these sayings of Mine, and does them, I will liken him to a wise man who built his house on the rock: and the rain descended, the floods came, and the winds blew and beat on that house; and it did not fall, for it was founded on the rock. But everyone who hears these sayings of Mine, and does not do them, will be like a foolish man who built his house on the sand: "and the rain descended, the floods came, and the winds blew and beat on that house; and it fell. And great was its fall.*
>
> —Matthew 7:24-27

If you are going to attempt to do anything for the Kingdom of God you will face resistance, trials, tribulation, and false accusations. The question is not will it come, but when it comes, what are you going to do? When tough times come, you need to be well-trained on your instrument panel (God's Word) so you will not rely on the flesh and crash and burn. The man who was not trained in the Word of God, built his house on the sand. When the storms came, his house was destroyed.

To realize the worth of the anchor, we need to feel the storm.

—Source Unknown

If you have ever been out on a fishing boat in a storm, you have learned this fact: A storm can cause you to become confused as to where you are and where you are going. God's Word is our compass in the midst of the storm. The compass of God's Word will lead you to shore safely. The Bible is your instrument panel and compass that will clearly guide you to what you must do to make it through a storm.

What to do When You Face a Crisis

You Must Examine Yourself

<u>Examine yourselves</u> as to whether you are in the faith. <u>Test yourselves</u>. Do you not know yourselves, that Jesus Christ is in you?—unless indeed you are disqualified.

—2 Corinthians 13:5
(Emphasis Added)

What do you need to do when you face a crisis? The first thing you must do is examine yourself. I am convinced that most Christians can get themselves into a lot of trouble, even without the devil's help. The Lord instructed Jonah to go to Nineveh. Instead of going to Nineveh, Jonah decided that he was going to go on a deep sea fishing trip to Tarpon Springs, Florida. Then he finds himself in the belly of a whale.

It is very important for you to notice that God prepared a crisis season for Jonah by doing two things: 1) God sent a vicious storm while they were out at sea (see Jonah 1:4). And 2)

God prepared and sent the whale to swallow Jonah (see Jonah 1:17). Please notice, it was not the devil who caused the crisis.

Now, if Jonah was like most Christians today, he would be in the belly of the whale doing a spiritual warfare dance saying, "I rebuke you devil, how dare you put me in this dark place. I bind you and cast you out—in Jesus' name!" The devil is scratching his head saying, "I did not put you in there, you did." Many people today are in the belly of the whale and they do not even know it. Why? Because God has called some men and women to usher, and they are not ushering. Others He has called to work the nursery and change baby diapers, but they are not doing it. Many people are called to clean the toilets and mow the grass of the church, while others are called to preach behind the pulpit. You were not saved to sit on the pew and smell like a pew. Most Christians know what they are saved *from,* but they don't know what they are saved *to.* You were saved *to serve.* The Bible says that your faith without *works* is dead (see James 2:26).

You do not have to be Jonah to have a crisis or trouble in your life. Just have a Jonah on the boat with you. It only takes one wrong person in your life to cause you a lot of trouble. One Jezebel spirit on the praise and worship team, one demon on your board, one wrong employee or staff member can wreck an entire ministry or business. Your crises season is a great sifter of wrong people. Don't be a pack rat of wrong people. Check out who you are hanging with. Are they in disobedience? The only thing you can do if you have a Jonah onboard is kick him off the boat. After Jonah was tossed overboard, the boat the storm calmed.

Crises are life's wake-up calls.

—Dick Leider

In the middle of Jonah's crisis, he went through a "process of change" in the belly of the whale. He turned the belly of the whale into a prayer closet. The pathway to getting out of the belly of the whale is through the doorway of repentance. When you repent, you reposition yourself for a miracle. Repentance also repositions you onto the road to your destiny. When Jonah finally obeyed the Lord and went to Nineveh, one of the greatest spiritual awakenings ever recorded in your Bible took place:

> *And Jonah began to enter the city on the first day's walk. Then he cried out and said, "Yet **forty days**, and Nineveh shall be overthrown!" So the people of Nineveh believed God, proclaimed a fast, and put on sackcloth, from the greatest to the least of them. Then God saw their works, that they turned from their evil way; and God relented from the disaster that He had said He would bring upon them, and He did not do it .*

> —Jonah 3:4-5,10
> (Emphasis Added)

Jonah embraced change in the process and then stepped into greatness. His prophetic warning of coming judgment caused an entire city to repent and experience a great awakening. There are many Jonahs today in the world who are running from the call of God. They are in the belly of the whale and are in the process of becoming a powerful mouthpiece for the Lord.

Everybody thinks of changing the world, but no one thinks of changing himself. —Leo Tolstoy

You Must Examine Your Calling

Thousands of born-again believers today are in the belly of the whale. God has called every person in the Kingdom to serve and use their talents (see Matthew 25:15-30). Bottom line, most Christians have caused their own crisis because they are not serving the Lord. Yes, you have been saved from a devil's hell, but you were also saved to serve in the Kingdom of God. When you refuse to walk in obedience to God's Word, you will find yourself in the belly of the whale and the pig pen of life. Stop blaming your church, pastor, spouse, friends, boss, and family for your crisis situation. Take responsibility and find something to do for the Lord who shed His blood for you. Take some time to get alone with God. Are you doing what He has called you to do? Showing up for church every Sunday is not enough. It is time for you to get busy serving in the Kingdom!

You Must Examine Your Belief System

The significant problems we face cannot be solved at the same level of thinking we were at when we created them.

—Albert Einstein

Crises seasons cause your mind to be open to new information. Dusty Bibles produce dirty people. Therefore, dusty Bibles produce dirty thinking. This is where we get the term "stinking thinking." The difference between *average* people and *effective* people is the information they posses. Average people are satisfied with the amount of information they have learned at this time. Successful and effective people are constantly looking for more information and revelation. I was not really convinced that God could heal my body until I needed a healing in my body. The crisis of sickness opened my mind to change what I believed so I could receive my healing. There was a song that I heard one time that said, "It's hard for me to admit I am wrong, until I realize that I cannot go on." This is a statement of truth according to Psalm 119:71, *"It is good for me that I have been **afflicted**, that I may **learn** Your statutes."*

You Cannot Change Your Life Until You Are Willing to Change Your Belief System

Wrong belief systems can hinder you from the abundant life Jesus has promised you. The Bible says in Romans 12:2, *"And do not be conformed to this world, but be **transformed** [changed] by the **renewing of your mind**, that you may prove what is that good and acceptable and perfect will of God."* You cannot change your life until you are willing to change your belief system. You will not be able to change your future unless you are willing to change your belief system. Renewing your mind is more than just learning a new truth. It is actually changing your actions and behavior. To begin the journey of renewing your mind, you have to come to a place in your life where you realize that your belief system is not 100 percent accurate.

What You Are Willing to Walk Away From Determines What GOD Can Bring into Your Life

For many years I would not give my life to Jesus Christ because I thought that being a Christian meant that I had to be poor. I received this wrong belief system by observing other Christians and by watching movies about Jesus on television. Hollywood always portrays Jesus and His disciples as being poverty stricken. Coming out of high school I had big dreams of becoming a wealthy business man, so I decided to wait on getting my life right.

A few years later, I gave my life to Jesus Christ, because I realized my need to be changed and forgiven of my sins. When I became born again, I started reading my Bible and began to find Scriptures concerning prosperity such as:

*His descendants will be mighty on earth; the generation of the upright will be blessed. **Wealth and riches** will be in his house, and his righteousness endures forever.*

—*Psalm 112:2-3*
(Emphasis Added)

*Let them shout for joy and be glad, who favor my righteous cause; and let them say continually, "Let the Lord be magnified, who has pleasure in the **prosperity** of His servant."*

—*Psalm 35:27*
(Emphasis Added)

*Beloved, I pray that you may **prosper** in all things and be in health, just as your soul prospers.*

—*3 John 2*
(Emphasis Added)

Belief Errors

I quickly realized that the devil had sold me a lie. God wanted me to prosper in every area of my life including financially. Some beliefs you now hold dearly are in error. No matter what you are going through today, you may be only one wrong belief system away from your next miracle.

Hosea 4:6 says, *"My people are destroyed for lack of knowledge."* The devil's success is based on your ignorance of the Word of God. Notice that the Bible does not say we perish because of a lack of money, a lack of miracles, or a lack of church attendance. We perish because of a lack of knowledge of the Word of God. This is why you need to become a daily student of the Word of God. The Bible tells us to, *"Study to shew thyself approved unto God, a workman that needeth not to be ashamed, rightly dividing the word of truth"* (2 Timothy 2:15 KJV).

You are currently only one revelation away from your breakthrough. A revelation is an explosion of truth from God's Word that breaks past the barriers of wrong thinking in your mind and becomes a living reality in your spirit. Jesus says in John, *"you shall know the truth, and the truth shall make you free"* (John 8:32).

Truth Forces Deception and Lies to the Surface

You see, truth (God's Word) forces wrong thinking to be revealed in your life. Truth forces deception and lies to surface. Truth always produces an atmosphere of liberty, faith, joy, and peace in your life. Lies and deception, or the works of the devil, always create an atmosphere of bondage, fear, depression, and confusion in your life. In this type of atmosphere you need to realize you are in spiritual warfare.

Truth is confrontational and will make you feel uncomfortable and even angry at times. You must learn to love and embrace truth in order to bring about the necessary changes and the blessings of God in your life. Warning: when you move toward the direction of change, get ready for resistance from the following areas: satan, world system, self, family, and "religious people."

Know Your Instrument Panel

*This book of the law shall not depart from your mouth, but you shall meditate in it **day and night** [**habit**], that you may observe to do according to all that is written in it. For then **you** will make **your** way prosperous, and then **you** will have good success.*

—*Joshua 1:8*
(Emphasis Added)

We all meditate every day. The question is, "What are you meditating on?" In order for you to experience your breakthrough, the Word of God must become the number one priority in your life. Many people put newspapers, magazines, and television shows before God's Word. Only God's Word produces right thinking, which produces success in your life.

Most people tend to make provision for failure, rather than preparation for success.

—*Source Unknown*

Your Success Is Up to You

When you meditate daily on the Word of God, you are inspired by the Holy Spirit to obey the Word. This causes you to be a *doer* of the Word and not a *hearer* only. Hearing alone is not faith. You must also act on the Word to be in 100 percent faith.

Notice the three "you's" in the last sentence of Joshua 1:8, *"For then **you** will make **your** way prosperous, and then **you** will have good success." You* removes the blame of failure from everything and everybody else. You can not blame the devil, God, race, spouse, or how you were raised. The determination of your success is up to you. You have a promise that if you will daily meditate on the Word and do what it says, **you** will make **your** way **prosperous** and have good success in every area of your life. Make a conscious decision in your heart to read the Bible daily. Do not forget to ask the Teacher of the universe, the Holy Spirit, to help you accomplish your goal.

The only real failure is not to learn.

—*Jimmy Carter*

We are living in a day when everybody wants to have an "experience" with God. However, a spiritual experience should never be a substitute for knowledge. You can have a wonderful experience with God, but live a life of total defeat. Why? Because you have not taken the time to obtain the wisdom of God. It takes time, effort, and hard work to obtain wisdom. Gaining wisdom is a result of reaching for spiritual laws, principles, and information from the Word of God. If all you needed was an experience with Jesus Christ, then there would be no need for the Bible.

Suppose you were facing a financial crisis. Would you need a $50,000 miracle or would you need wisdom? The answer: wisdom. Why? Because if God gave you $50,000 today without wisdom, you would most likely spend it foolishly on wrong things. Then you would need another miracle to pull you out of another crisis.

The Devil's Biggest Fear

Truth coming into your life is the biggest fear of the devil. Why? Because he can no longer take advantage of you in the area of your weakness. All of us have problem areas in our lives that we seem to battle on a regular basis. To overcome these weaknesses, we must energize our spirit with truth

(God's Word) in that particular area of our lives. Hebrews 4:12 says, *"For the word of God is living and **powerful**, and sharper than any two-edged sword...."* One of the meanings for the word *powerful* in the Greek is *energy*. God's Word will supernaturally energize you to walk victoriously in any area of your life.

I had an anger problem; so to overcome it throughout the day, I would constantly meditate on James 1:19, *"So then, my beloved brethren, let every man be swift to hear, slow to speak, slow to wrath."* When I was tempted in that area, I was energized with God's Word so I could overcome my weakness and walk in love.

The road to success is always under construction.

—*Willie Gray*

Four Steps to Lasting Change

Here is how the great A.W. Tozer advised people on how to change their lives: "Try what I call the pad and pencil method. This method is very simple and consists of getting on your hands and knees with your Bible, a pad of paper and a pencil. Read the Bible and then write down what is wrong with you."

Step 1—Recognize the wrong belief system you have.

And saying, Repent (think differently; change your mind, regretting your sins and changing your conduct), for the kingdom of heaven is at hand.
—*Matthew 3:2 AMP*

Take time and ask yourself, "What do I really think and believe?" Many people do not even know what they believe.

Admit your belief system can be wrong and be willing to change. Change is good and change brings growth.

Step 2—Know your weaknesses.

He who covers his sins will not prosper, but whoever confesses and forsakes them will have mercy.

—*Proverbs 28:13*

In what area or areas of your life are you constantly being defeated? Be honest with yourself. The devil already knows your weaknesses—do you? The weakness or sin you fail to deal with, could eventually be your downfall.

Step 3—Have a truth explosion.

Your Word is a lamp to my feet and a light to my path.

—*Psalm 119:105*

"Is not My word like a fire?" says the Lord, "And like a hammer that breaks the rock in pieces?"

—*Jeremiah 23:29*

Find out what God's Word says about your situation, weaknesses, or wrong belief systems. God's Word will shine the light on these hindrances and will force the darkness to be revealed and destroyed.

Step 4—Daily feed your spirit.

Your Word I have hidden in my heart, that I might not sin against You.

—*Psalm 119:11*

Memorize, pray, and boldly confess God's Word until your mind and spirit come in agreement with the Word. Jesus overcame every lie of the devil with this statement: "It is written! It is written! It is written!" If the devil has been bothering you, do what Jesus did and overcome him by speaking what the Word says out of your mouth. It is written!

You Must Examine Your Speech

Put your mind in gear before you put your tongue in motion!

—Source Unknown

Your words are deciding your tomorrow. Successful leadership within the home, community, workplace, church, or business depends on the words you use. It is imperative that you recognize and understand the danger of the tongue. Your words during a crisis can influence the course of your life in the same way that a small rudder can influence the course of a great ship.

*Look also at ships: although they are so large and are driven by fierce winds, they are turned by a very small rudder wherever the pilot desires. Even so the tongue is a little member and boasts great things. See how great a forest a little fire kindles! And the tongue is a fire, a world of iniquity. **The tongue** is so set among our members that it defiles the whole body, and **sets on fire the course of nature**; and it is set on fire by hell.*

—James 3:4-6

David knew that there was great danger in speaking wrong things. He had great concerns for his own tongue during adverse circumstances, *"LORD, who may abide in Your tabernacle? Who may dwell in Your holy hill? He who **does not backbite** with his tongue, nor does evil to his neighbor, nor does he take up a reproach against his friend"* (Psalm 15:1,3). And, *"Who is the man who desires life, and loves many days, that **he may see good? Keep your tongue from evil**, and your lips from speaking deceit"* (Psalm 34:12-13).

You can create your own crisis by the words you speak out of your own mouth. Refuse to talk bad about, complain, or backbite about your pastor and church. Watch out for what you say about yourself, family, boss, and co-workers. Stop making statements like, "I'm catching the flu," "I'll always be poor," "Everything bad always happens to me," "I'm a failure," "I'm stupid," "I'll never get ahead in life," etc. If you say these type of things often enough, you will believe them and they will come true.

Here are three suggestions I heard from Pastor Charles Swindoll on the radio about how to keep your tongue in check:

> **1.** Think before you speak.
>
> **2.** Talk less.
>
> **3.** Start today! Install the muzzle now.

David said the same thing in Psalm 39:1, *"I said, 'I will guard my ways, Lest I sin with my tongue; I will restrain my mouth with a muzzle, while the wicked are before me.'"*

God created you in His image. You have within yourself the creative abilities of God. What you say can be a creative force that cannot be turned around. *"You are snared by the words of your mouth; you are taken by the words of your mouth"* (Proverbs 6:2).

You are a prophet over your own life. Are you speaking words of victory or defeat? Success or failure? Health or sickness? Abundance or poverty? When you change your confession, you will change your direction and move forward toward success and overcome every crisis.

CHAPTER FIVE

THE PRAISE ZONE

I will never forget the many different struggles my wife and I had to face while pastoring our first church. One time, I had just finished preaching and teaching a sermon on the responsibility we have as Christians to daily walk in love and forgiveness toward other people. At the end of the message, I asked everybody in the church to go to one another and ask for forgiveness over any harm or hurt they may have caused toward another. My wife and I proceeded into the congregation to greet and to love on the people. Suddenly, a young teenager in the church ran up to me and said, "Two men are fist fighting in the front yard of the church!" By the time I was able to get outside, both men were in their cars driving away. I telephoned both men and scheduled a time the next day to talk to them.

The man who initiated the fight opened the office visit by telling me that the Lord had spoken to him that night about our church and about my pastoral leadership. He then listed a number of things that he thought was wrong with me, my wife, and several different people in our church. I then asked the man a question, "What did the Lord tell you about your actions yesterday?" This caused the man to explode in anger. He stormed out of my office and then spread vicious rumors about our ministry. This man caused such a ruckus that the following Sunday over one half of our congregation did not attend services.

The following month I had scheduled a revival meeting with a very popular traveling evangelist. I called the evangelist and told him that I had to cancel the event because of the church split. The evangelist said, "When you have something bad happen in your church...that is when you need a move of God the most." I agreed to continue with the scheduled meetings.

I remember how hard it was for me to go into the services and see only a fraction of the people present. My wife and I had worked so hard to build up that little struggling country church. The offerings were drastically reduced. The morale of the church was at an all-time low. I really wanted to just quit the ministry.

The next week the evangelist sent me a confirmation letter and at the end of the letter he closed with, "Stay in the Praise Zone!" I instantly knew what I was supposed to do. For the next three weeks, I decided that I was going to praise God no matter what my outward circumstances looked like. In each service, I intentionally led our worship team into four or five more songs. When the evangelist arrived, the revival meeting turned out fabulously. We gained several new members and experienced a tremendous jump in our monthly income. More importantly, the second principle I learned in the classroom of crisis was to maintain a lifestyle of praise and worship during difficult times.

When David was in serious trouble with King Achish in Gath, he escaped by pretending to be insane (see 1 Samuel 21:10-15). David composed the following song after he escaped:

*I will bless the LORD at all times; His praise shall **continually** be in my mouth. My soul shall make its boast in the LORD; the humble shall hear of it and be glad. Oh, **magnify** the LORD with me, and let us exalt His name together. I sought the LORD, and He heard me, and delivered me from all my fears.*

—*Psalm 34:1-4*
(Emphasis Added)

In times of trouble, you must learn to bless the Lord. No matter what you are going through, you must keep a song in your heart and on your lips. You have got to learn to praise God during both the mountaintop and valley seasons. When things are going good and when everything around you seems to be falling apart—praise the Lord.

I love when David says, "Oh, *magnify*...." What do you do when you magnify something? You make it bigger. The word *magnify* in this Scripture verse means just that, make God bigger and enlarge Him. When you praise the Lord, you make God bigger. I want you to know that you serve a big and an awesome God, and there is a little bitty devil. When you praise God, you make God bigger than your problems and bigger than the devil.

During our services I encourage people to praise the Lord. Many times I will look over the crowd and most of the people are just standing there looking at me like a deer looks at the headlights of a car in the middle of the highway. You are not praising the Lord unless your lips are moving, *"Therefore by*

*Him let us continually offer the sacrifice of praise to God, that is, the **fruit of our lips**, giving thanks to His name"* (Hebrews 13:15).

When you continually praise the Lord on a daily basis and throughout the day, you learn to live in the Praise Zone. The goal of a football team is to continually get into the end zone. The end zone represents a place of victory, excitement, celebration, and great joy. In the same way, the Praise Zone is a place of victory, excitement, celebration, and great joy.

The only weapon the devil has is his voice (1 Peter 5:8). He has no power or authority, only the power of suggestion and a bunch of tricks. Your praise creates an atmosphere that silences your adversary. *"Out of the mouth of babes and nursing infants You have ordained strength, because of Your enemies, that You may silence the enemy and the avenger"* (Psalm 8:2). When you praise and worship the Lord, you create a restrictive zone of the presence of the Lord all around you. At a crime scene the officers mark off the area with yellow tape, restricting entrance into the area. This zone becomes a restricted area. In the same way, the enemy's voice cannot penetrate the Praise Zone. In the Praise Zone you hear the voice of the Father say, "This is My Son in whom I am well pleased." In the Praise Zone you will have joy, strength, protection, peace, and healing. Therefore, your praise creates an invisible protective force all around you.

Recognizing the Three Zones

The Praise Zone

- ⮞ Praise is continual (Heb. 13:15).

- ⮞ God is bigger than any problem.

- ⮞ Problems dissipate. Joy, peace, protection, and healing reign.

The Struggle Zone

➲ Praise only occasionally (Psalm 42:5).

➲ Constant struggle.

➲ Wavering faith producing fatigue.

➲ Times of joy and peace and times of misery and confusion.

The Dead Zone

➲ Never praise (Psalm 115:17).

➲ Problems are bigger than God.

➲ Defeated, victim mentality, no joy or peace, and no faith.

People who only *occasionally* praise the Lord live in what I call the Struggle Zone. In this zone a person is in a constant struggle with themselves and others. They are what I call Yo-Yo Christians. They are up one day and down the next. They are walking in faith one minute and the next minute they want to quit and give up. Why? Because the enemy's voice has not been silenced in their lives. They hear the voice of the Holy Spirit say, "You *are* going to make it. Everything is going to be all right." Then they hear the voice of the devil say, "You're a failure. God is not going to come through for you. Just quit." This type of inner struggle produces fatigue, robs you of your joy, and depletes you of peace.

Another group of people live in the Dead Zone. The Bible says, *"The dead do not praise the LORD, nor any who go down into silence"* (Psalm 115:17). Spiritually dead people *never* praise the Lord. They go to church, but they have not learned the power of praise. Therefore, they live defeated, faithless, miserable, and confused lives.

Thanksgiving, praise, worship, and prayer moves you into a place of intimacy with God. Intimacy with God is the highest form of spiritual warfare. Many Christians talk more to the devil than they do to the Lord. The Bible teaches us that there is a place where we can go in God that the enemy cannot touch us.

> *We know that whoever is born of God does not sin; but he who has been born of God keeps himself, and the **wicked one does not touch him**.*
>
> —1 John 5:18
> (Emphasis Added)

The Secret Place

David describes that place as the Secret Place, *"He who dwells in **the secret place** of the Most High shall abide under the shadow of the Almighty. I will say of the LORD, 'He is my refuge and my fortress; my God, in Him I will trust.' Surely He shall deliver you from the snare of the fowler* [enemy] *and from the perilous pestilence"* (Psalm 91:1-3).

When everything in David's life seemed to be falling apart, he learned to run to the Secret Place.

> *One thing I have desired of the LORD, That will I seek: That I may dwell in the house of the LORD All the days of my life, to behold the beauty of the LORD, And to inquire in His temple. For in the **time of trouble** He shall hide me in His pavilion; **in the secret place** of His tabernacle He shall hide me; He shall set me high upon a rock."* \
>
> —Psalm 27:4-5
> (Emphasis Added)

In the Secret Place, God becomes bigger than any problem you will ever face. You do not have to fight your battles alone, just allow God to show up on your battlefield—He will help you fight your battles.

In Times of Trouble, Stay in the Praise Zone

The Bible describes the zone of the presence of the Lord as a pavilion, fortress, shadow, hedge, rock, a covering of feathers, and a shield. Let's look at a definition of all seven examples:

PAVILION - *"For in the time of trouble He shall hide me in His **pavilion**..."* (Psalm 27:5). A pavilion is a large open-sided tent or shelter. What is a shelter? A shelter is a covering that protects you from a storm or the heat of the sun. A pavilion creates a zone over a person. This covering keeps the elements from hitting or hurting you.

FORTRESS - *"I will say of the LORD, 'He is my refuge and my **fortress**...'"* (Psalm 91:2). A fortress is a place permanently fortified for defense. A fortress or fort is designed to keep the enemy out and to protect all those who are inside. If you stay inside the fortress, you remain in a protective zone.

ROCK – *"The LORD is my **rock** and my fortress and my deliverer; my God, my strength, in whom I will trust; my shield and the horn of my salvation, my stronghold"* (Psalm 18:2). When thinking of the biblical land, it is important not to forget that rocks formed part of their daily living. Floridians know sand and swamps, Georgians know red clay, and biblical land people knew rocks very well. Old Testament writers thought of rocks as the "ultimate haven," a place of refuge and protection. It was in rocky mountains where natural caverns provided a "safety zone" against the elements of nature, intruders, and invaders.

SHADOW - *"...Shall abide under the **shadow** of the Almighty"* (Psalm 91:1). A shadow is an outlined figure of an object when it intercepts the light. A shadow provides protection from the sunlight. On a hot summer day, the shadow of an oak tree provides protection from the sunlight. If you stay in the Shadow Zone, you will be protected from the blistering heat of the sun.

FEATHERS - *"He shall **cover you** with His **feathers**, and under His wings you shall take refuge..."* (Psalm 91:4). I was fishing one day and I saw a duck sitting on the shoreline. About fifteen minutes latter, I glanced over at the duck again. Suddenly, I saw several little ducklings come out from under the duck's wings. Mama's wings covered the ducklings from the visual sight of their enemy. In the Secret Place, God hides you in an invisible zone from the view of your adversaries. This is why David says of God, *"You are my hiding place; You shall preserve me from trouble; You shall surround me with songs of deliverance. Selah"* (Psalm 32:7).

HEDGE – *"Have You not made a **hedge** around him, around his household, and around all that he has on every side? You have blessed the work of his hands, and his possessions have increased in the land"* (Job 1:10). A hedge is row of bushes or shrubs grown closely together to create a fence. What do fences do? They form a zone that forbids entry by unwanted people or animals. How did Job create this hedge? He would rise early every morning and give God a sacrifice (see Job 1:5).

SHIELD - *"But You, O LORD, are a **shield** for me, my glory and the One who lifts up my head"* (Psalm 3:3, see also Psalm 28:7, Deuteronomy 33:29). A shield is a defensive device usually used by a soldier. They can be as large as a door or small and round. A shield can be simply anything that protects by warding off harm or danger. If you are standing behind the shield, you are in a safety zone.

How to Stay in the Praise Zone?

You must decide to make praise and worship part of your daily lifestyle. You were created to praise and worship the Lord, *"But you are a chosen generation, a royal priesthood, a holy nation, His own special people, **that you may proclaim the praises of Him** who called you out of darkness into His marvelous light"* (1 Peter 2:9).

This is not something you do only when you go to church on Sunday morning. David says, *"Seven times a day I praise You, because of Your righteous judgments* (Psalm 119:164). Here is an example of how you can praise the Lord seven times a day. Praise Him:

1. First thing in the morning.

2. When you are taking a shower.

3. When eating your breakfast.

4. During your break at work.

5. When eating your lunch.

6. During dinnertime.

7. Before you go to bed.

Praise the Lord regardless of the circumstances you face and regardless how you feel. You have a choice every day. You can complain and remain or praise and raise. The choice is yours.

Just Cry!

In the summer of 1997, we set up a 600-seat tent in Central Park in Rochester, New York. Each night the tent was filled with prostitutes, drug addicts, alcoholics, and small children experiencing the transforming power and love of Jesus Christ. This meeting has now grown into a 200-member church. We were on such a spiritual high when we came home from those meetings!

When we arrived home, the next three weeks of meetings that I had scheduled were suddenly canceled by the pastors for very weird reasons. To make matters worse, we then had to face a stack of bills on my desk that needed to be paid right away. My wife started to cry, "How are we going to pay all these bills?" For the first time in my life I did not have an answer for her. So I cried with her. Yes, God's man of great faith and power cried. A phone call interrupted our pity party. I was crying so hard that my wife went into another room to answer the phone.

When I finally stopped crying, the Holy Spirit instantly told me to call three pastors. I called each pastor and instantly booked the next three weeks with meetings. If you have never been in traveling ministry, you will never know what a true miracle this was.

This life experience taught me the third principle in the classroom of crisis, which is to "just cry" during difficult times.

*When the righteous **cry** for help, the*
LORD hears, and delivers them out
of all their distress and troubles.

—Psalm 34:17 AMP
(Emphasis Added)

God responds to the cry of His children when they are facing crises, trouble, and adversity. If you have ever been a parent, then you have experienced the communication system of a baby. What do babies do when they have wet diapers or if they are hungry? They simply cry. The cry of the child causes parents to stop what they are doing and move toward meeting the needs of their baby. In the same way, when you cry out to God, He moves toward meeting your needs.

Blind Bartimaeus did not pray the perfect prayer when Jesus was passing by. He simply cried out "Jesus, Son of David, have mercy on me." The religious people told him to be quiet, which caused Bartimaeus to cry out even louder. Then the Bible says that "Jesus stood still," and healed him (see Luke 18:25-41). There is something about your cry that captures the Lord's attention. You see, your cry has to become louder than the hush of others and the devil. If the devil cannot hush you up, he cannot keep you down. The crisis season will motivate you to cry out to God in a biblical way.

Cry out to God:

⮑ With your voice, *"I cried to the LORD with my voice, and He heard me from His holy hill. Selah"* (Psalm 3:4).

⮑ Daily during a crisis, *"Be merciful to me, O Lord, for I cry to You all day long"* (Psalm 86:3).

⮑ In humility, *"When He avenges blood, He remembers them; He does not forget the cry of the humble"* (Psalm 9:12).

⮑ In praise, *"When I cry out to You, Then my enemies will turn back; this I know, because God is for me. In God (I will praise His word), in the LORD (I will praise His word)"* (Psalm 56:9-10).

We should cry out loudly. The intensity of the cry of the child determines how quickly the parent responds. This is also true in crying out to God, the perfect Father and Parent. Your tears touch the heart of God. He will respond to your cry. Your tears are like liquid prayer petitions before the Lord. The Lord reads your tears. If you learn to weep before Him, you will not weep before your enemies.

Stop acting like you have it all together. Instead, humble yourself and cry out to God for deliverance.

CHAPTER SIX

YOUR DREAM WILL PULL YOU OUT!

Do not deliver me to the will of my adversaries;
for false witnesses have risen against me, and such
as breathe out violence. I would have lost heart,
unless I had believed that I would see the goodness
of the LORD in the land of the living.

—Psalm 27:12-13

You will discover in this Scripture from Psalm 27 the fourth thing you need to do to successfully lead in crisis times. This is a psalm David wrote when he was in the middle of a crisis, when the pressure was the greatest, and he was on the brink of giving up. In the midst of his trouble he was "losing heart." During this difficult time, David decided to believe that he would see the goodness of the Lord in his future. Not in the great by and by, but in the here and now. The dream of a better tomorrow motivated David to not give up in his present condition. The success of your dream and your future lies in your ability *to see beyond what is to what will be.*

Thinking and dreaming about your future is a necessity for making it through the struggle seasons of life. Most people rarely dream about their future. Why? Because most people are so focused on trying to fix their immediate problems.

It is hard to think about the future when you are in a swamp and up to your neck in alligators!

—Source Unknown

Dreaming about the future creates excitement and energy. Focusing on your present failures, setbacks, and disappointments is depressing and energy draining. In the valley season you need all the excitement and energy that you can get.

In a twenty-year period, you can accomplish almost anything you desire. Just consider: Once U.S. leaders made up their minds, they needed only eight years to put a man on the moon. America's richest man in 1995, Bill Gates, was nearly penniless in 1975. Japan was an isolated, backward, dirt-poor nation in the nineteenth century. But it became a world power in just a few decades. How did all these accomplishments come to pass? By deliberately refusing to look at present conditions and by dreaming of a great new future for itself.[1]

You are somewhere in the future and you are looking much better than you look right now.

—Kim Clement

You must continually keep your eyes focused on your future. Focusing on your current circumstances will only depress and drain you of energy. God created you with two eyes. He intentionally located your eyes on the front of your head. You were naturally created to look forward. You may be feeling like a slave to your present, but you can control your future. You must start looking ahead, dreaming, thinking, planning, and acting today. You can build a great future for your life. The time to start is now!

**If there's hope in the future there
is power in the present.**

—John Maxwell

I believe that it was Joseph's dream of being in the palace that motivated him not to give up and quit while he was in the pit and the prison. Holding onto your dream during a crisis will pull you out of every valley season.

Everybody has a dream. A dream is something that you want to see happen in the future. The Book of Hebrews tells us to, *"...hold fast the confession of our hope without wavering, for He who promised is faithful* (Hebrews 10:23). Paul encourages us to "hold fast the confession of our hope." True Bible hope is different from the world's definition of hope. Hope is not wishing, rubbing a rabbit's foot, or even crossing your fingers. True Bible hope is a positive, confident, red hot, burning, earnest expectation with an outstretched neck that something good is going to happen to you in your future. Hope confidently believes that the days ahead of you are going to be the best days of your life.

Do Not Let Go of Your Dream

In the Greek, "hold fast" means to hold on tightly and with extreme force. Picture a child holding onto a door knob wanting to go outside. The mother is trying to pull the child away from the door knob. The child refuses to let go and holds on so tightly that his feet are lifted off the floor. Can you picture that? You must hold on to your dreams with the same "bull dog" tenacity!

God has great plans for you in spite of your capabilities and your incapabilities. He has great plans for you even if you have stopped believing in yourself, God, and others. The Lord has great plans for you in the face of the negative messages in your past and present. Your future is looking much better than you can ever imagine. How do I know? Because God's Word says so! You have a promise in Jeremiah 29:11, *"For I know the thoughts that I think toward you, says the LORD, thoughts of peace* [or prosperity] *and not of evil, to give you a future and a hope."*

Do not allow the enemy to tell you that you do not have a dream or a great future. Even if you do not think that you have a dream, you do. God did not forget you when He was passing out dreams. You do have a dream and it already exists. The dream has been there from the day of your conception *"Your eyes saw my substance, being yet unformed. And in Your book they all were written, the days fashioned for me, when as yet there were none of them"* (Psalm 139:16).

Every person God created has the potential to make a great impact in this world.

The key to making a powerful impact is found when you discover your dream. To discover your dream you must stop looking outward and start looking inward. The Bible says that God will give you the desires of your heart. (See Psalm 20:4; 21:2; 37:4; Proverbs 10:24.) Who do you think put the desires in your heart? God. Your heart knows things that your mind, logic, and education do not know. Solomon says in Proverbs, *"The **heart** knows its own bitterness, and a stranger does not share its joy"* (Proverbs 14:10). Most people try to figure out their destinies with their minds, but all your dreams reside in your heart, not in your head. Discovering your destiny is a matter of discovering your true heart desires.

Take time to dream, think, and reflect. Most people are so action-oriented that they do not take time to just sit down and dream. Here are some questions to ask yourself. They will help you discover the true desires of your heart:

- ➲ What do you dream of accomplishing?
- ➲ What were some of your childhood dreams?
- ➲ What do you like?
- ➲ What do you hate?
- ➲ What excites you?
- ➲ What are your three greatest talents?
- ➲ What do others say you are good at?
- ➲ What do you want to be remembered for?
- ➲ What would you attempt for the Lord if you knew it was impossible to fail?

Do not answer these questions with your mind, listen to your heart.

If you are going to have a dream, make sure you have a large one. Make your dream so big that without God's help, it will be impossible for you to fulfill. The bigger you make your dream, the more of yesterday's hurts, failures, and tragedies you will forget. Why? Because you will be so consumed in working to accomplish your dream, you will not have time to think about your past.

**There can't be a crisis next week.
My schedule is already full.**

—*Henry Kissinger*

Development Stages

A dream is a seed that God plants in the fertile soil of your heart. Every seed God plants, He always expects to get a harvest. God wants your dreams to come to pass. Your harvest or dreams will not come overnight. When you sow a seed, the seed must go through a process of development before you see the actual produce of the seed. In the same way, your dream will go through a process of development before you will see any results.

The story of the conception of Mary, the mother of Jesus Christ is a great example of the process and development period of any dream or promise from God. The first stage is the time of conception.

Stage 1—Conception

The Angel of the Lord appeared to Mary and told her that she would conceive in her womb and bring forth a Son, and shall call His name Jesus. At first, Mary was puzzled because she was a virgin. Then the angel said to her *"...The Holy Spirit will come upon you, and the power of the Highest will overshadow you; therefore, also, that Holy One who is to be born will be called the Son of God"* (Luke 1:35). Mary did not consult her mind or logic concerning this supernatural experience. She had a concise word from the Lord concerning her future.

Look at her response, *"Behold the maidservant of the Lord! Let it be to me according to your word"* (Luke 1:38). At that moment, Mary became pregnant with promise. God was doing a new thing on the earth and Mary listened to the *rhema* word from God. She simply believed that through her body the Son of God would be born.

You must start your dream with a clear and direct word from God. Your dream must be conceived before it can be achieved. Your dream cannot be just a "good idea." Do not attempt to achieve a dream or a goal that God did not instruct you to pursue. Wrong dreams and goals can become substitutes for right dreams and goals.

Stage 2—Development/Process

If you think the next nine months of Mary's life was easy, you are completely wrong. Can you imagine how many people mocked her? Accused her of getting pregnant out of wedlock. Laughed at the story that she conceived the child by the Holy Spirit. Can you imagine what it would be like telling her father and mother that she was pregnant?

While the baby grows in the womb, the mother becomes very uncomfortable. Many people today feel like they are outside of God's will when they feel uncomfortable. However, that which is birthed by the Holy Spirit will start to grow. The growth of the baby will naturally cause discomfort. The growth of your dream will also cause you to feel uncomfortable at times.

During the duration of a mother's pregnancy, the mother must guard and protect her body and the baby. She has to watch what she eats, drinks, and does to her body. The mother must be careful not to overwork herself. She must guard herself from participating in activities that may cause harm to her and the baby. One wrong move during the baby's development stage can mess up the child's entire life.

The development process is the most important time to protect your dream from those who are *spiritual abortionists.* There are five spiritual abortionists that you must guard yourself against.

Spiritual Abortionist 1—Time

There is a long period of time between the birth of your dream and its full manifestation. Time has a way of wearing on us. Remember, delay is not denial! Rome was not built in a day. Your dream does not have an expiration date. Give your dream and vision at least five years to develop. Knowing this delivers you from the "American Instantism" mentality.

Keep on going and the chances are you will stumble on something, perhaps when you are least expecting it. I have never heard of anyone stumbling on something sitting down.

—Charles F. Kettering

Spiritual Abortionist 2—The Devil

The devil will resist you. Why? Because the fulfillment of your assignment will cause great embarrassment to the kingdom of darkness. Resistance is the proof that your miracle is on the way.

Spiritual Abortionist 3—
People: Family, Friends and Work Associates

I heard a preacher say one time that "The devil does not come to church wearing a red suit with horns, and carrying a pitch fork in his hand. He comes to church wearing a double-breasted suit with a necktie or a nice, pretty dress." The enemy will sometimes use those close to you to get you to abort your dreams. The world is full of non-achievers who will tell you to retreat and quit.

> **The great joy in life is actually doing**
> **what people say that you cannot do.**
>
> —*Mario Murillo*

Spiritual Abortionist 4—Yourself

The biggest enemy is sometimes—*me!* Keep your attitude positive. Your attitude is the determining factor between success and failure. The attitude of the leader in any organization will be a barometer of the attitude of the people. Positive leaders produce positive followers. Your attitude will either draw people to you or push them away from you. Attitudes are contagious—is yours worth catching? Even God cannot help those who insist on maintaining a negative attitude. Remember, winners never quit and quitters never win.

Spiritual Abortionist 5—Habits, Routine, and Ruts

Habits are formed by continually doing the same thing over and over. A habit becomes something that you can do without thinking. Your habits can kill your ability to dream. Why? Because when you stop thinking, you stop dreaming. People who are creatures of habit become mechanical, predictable, and stop desiring change. Habits, routine, and ruts stifle your creativity.

Write Your Dream!

Helen Keller was asked, "What would be worse than being born blind?" She replied, "To have sight with no vision." It is imperative that you take the time to write out your dreams and goals in life, *"Then the LORD answered me and said: 'Write the vision and make it plain on tablets, that he may run who reads it. For the vision is yet for an appointed time; but at the end it will speak, and it will not lie. Though it tarries, wait for it; because it will surely come, it will not tarry* (Habakkuk 2:2-3). Your dream is only a thought until you put it down on paper. Don't just dream it, ink it. This will help you keep your focus when the "spiritual abortionists" and the storms of life come against you.

Turn Your Dream into a Plan

Henry Ford, at the age of forty, was working in a garage. He was miserable and dissatisfied. One day he had an idea of how to mass produce automobiles on an assembly line.

➲ He had a dream.

➲ He planned his steps.

➲ He worked his plan.

Within twenty years, Henry Ford went from being a garage employee to being one of the wealthiest men in the world. This all happened because he had a dream, he wrote down a plan, and he stuck with it.

Give me a stock clerk with a goal, and I will give you a man who will make history. Give me a man without a goal and I will give you a stock clerk.

—*J.C. Penney*

Hold on to the Promises of God

In the midst of the development process, you must learn to hold on to the promises of God. How can you hold on to these promises if you do not know what they are? It is important for you to know the exact Scripture and verse for every promise that you are believing God for. Seasons change, but God's promises to you will never change. Look what Paul says about the promises of God, *"For all the promises of God in Him are Yes, and in Him Amen, to the glory of God through us* (2 Corinthians 1:20). God has answered every question concerning every promise you are believing Him for. The answer is always *yes!*

Have you ever thought, *Will I ever fulfill my destiny?* The answer is *yes!* Why? Because you have a promise from God in Philippians 1:6, *"Being confident of this very thing, that He who has begun a good work in you will **complete it** until the day of Jesus Christ."*

Maybe you are in a financial bind and you are thinking, *Is God going to supply my financial needs?* The answer again is *yes!* Why? You have another promise, *"And my God shall supply all your need according to His riches in glory by Christ Jesus"* (Philippians 4:19).

Continue to stand on the promises of God for your dream, healing, deliverance, family, and your finances. Don't give up now! Your miracle is on the way, *"But without faith it is impossible to please Him, for he who comes to God must believe that He is, and that **He is a rewarder** of those who diligently seek Him* (Hebrews 11:6). God rewards those who refuse to take *no* as an answer from the devil, and takes *yes* as the answer to every promise from God.

Stage 3—Manifestation

Just before the manifestation of your dream, things will get intense, painful, and messy. Mary and Joseph faced a setback when they could not find a room at the inn to have their baby. A mother's water will break just prior to the birth of a baby. This is a messy sight. The closer the time comes when a baby will be born, the more intense the pressure and pain. However, the mother must push during this process. Likewise, spiritual warfare will always surround the birth of your miracle. The spirit of discouragement will try to rob you of the confidence you need to face the challenges before you. You must rise above your discouragements at once and push through!

The fortitude of a man is measured by his resistance to become discouraged.

—*Source Unknown*

Harlan (Colonel) Sanders faced a crisis at the age of 66. He lost his business and had to live on only his social security check. His social security check was not enough, so he went around the country trying to sell his recipe for fried chicken. He was rejected 1,009 times before someone finally said yes. He went on to become a multimillionaire at an age when most people are quitting.[2]

Here's the good news! The fact that you have a mess is proof that your dream is about to manifest. You may have tried 1,008 times. Do not give up now. You have been carrying this dream for too long. On the 1,009th time, you may see your breakthrough manifested. Keep pushing until you see the promise with your eyes and touch it with your hands. What an exciting time to be alive! You stand today at the beginning of a new season when every promise you have from God is about to come to pass. I believe that your time of waiting is about over. Your miracle is about to be manifested in the natural realm.

Keep Your Focus

The enemy will try to break your focus to fulfill your God-given dreams, plans, and destiny for your life. Broken focus has been the downfall of many great men and women of God. How does the enemy try to get you to break your focus? By using distractions. Adam and Eve were distracted by the enemy and the forbidden fruit. David was distracted by Bathsheba, and Samson was distracted by Delilah. Judas was distracted by money.

Golf immortal Arnold Palmer recalls a lesson that he learned: "It was the final hole of the 1961 Masters tournament, and I had a one-stroke lead and had just hit a very satisfying tee shot. I felt I was in pretty good shape. As I approached my ball, I saw an old friend standing at the edge of the gallery. He motioned me over, stuck out his hand and said, 'Congratulations.' I took his hand and shook it, but as soon as I did, I knew I had lost my focus. On my next two shots, I hit the ball into a sand trap, then put it over the edge of the green. I missed a putt and lost the Masters. You don't forget a mistake like that; you just learn from it and become determined that you will never do that again. I haven't in the 30 years since."[3]

Great men and women of God have great focus. David was a great worshiper because he identified what was important to him. David was focused on living in the presence of God; ***One thing*** *I have desired of the LORD, that will I seek: That I may dwell in the house of the LORD all the days of my life, to behold the beauty of the LORD, and to inquire in His temple* (Psalm 27:4).

The apostle Paul was a great man of focus, *"Brethren, I do not count myself to have apprehended; but **one thing** I do, forgetting those things which are behind and reaching forward to those things which are ahead"* (Philippians 3:13).

Jesus Christ mastered focus when He went to the cross:

"Looking unto Jesus, the author and finisher of our faith, who for the joy that was set before Him endured the cross, despising the shame, and has sat down at the right hand of the throne of God."

—Hebrews 12:2

Starting to Finish

A decade ago, *Quote* magazine carried this story about one man's amazing persistence. The nations of the world had gathered for the Olympic games. Athletes from around the globe had trained for years to compete in the games and finally the time had arrived. The marathon, while not always exciting to watch, is surely the most severe Olympic test of human endurance. Many runners trained extensively to compete. The race began and eventually, the winner came running back into the Olympic stadium, welcomed by cheers from appreciative fans. Soon other runners arrived as well and eventually, the race was over.

The race was over except for one runner. A single, lone runner was still out on the course. Other track events continued in the stadium and an hour passed. Then two. Finally several hours later, the final runner, an athlete from Tanzania, entered the stadium. His pace was slow. His steps were wobbly. His knee was bloody and bandaged from a fall earlier in the race. He looked absolutely terrible; but as he entered the stadium, the fans realized who he was and what he was doing and began to cheer. As he made his way around the track and finally, painfully, across the finish line, the cheers swelled as the fans saluted the man's determination.

Later, after the race, the runner was asked why, even though he had lost the race by several hours, he had continued running. His answer was simple: *"My country did not send me 7,000 miles away to start the race. They sent me 7,000 miles to finish it."*

You will be known for what you finish, not for what you start. Finishing means training, self-denial and staying focused on your dreams and goals. God has not put you here to start. He has put you here to finish!

If your focus is on the negative, all you will see and experience is the agony of defeat. If you are focused on being a winner, you will see opportunities where you used to see brick walls. If you are focused on being positive, you will see rainbows instead of hurricanes. If you will learn to focus on your future, you will come to a place one day where you are actually living your dream.

ENDNOTES

1. Edward Cornish, "Exploring Your Future," *World Future Society 2000*, 5-6.

2. Robert T. Kiyosaki with Sharon L. Lechter, *Rich Dad, Poor Dad* (New York: Warner Books 2000), 156.

3. Carol Mann, "The 19th Hole" (Longmeadow), quoted in *Reader's Digest*.

CHAPTER SEVEN

LIVING BIG IN SMALL PLACES

*Though your beginning was small, yet your latter end would **increase** abundantly*

—Job 8:7
(Emphasis Added)

This Scripture from Job will pull you through every crisis, trial, and setback that you will ever face in life. These words were spoken to Job when he had lost everything. Job suffered the greatest calamities of anyone in the Bible. In a short period of time, his entire world came tumbling down. When you have no money, no children, a wife who is angry at you, and bad health, you are facing a set of crises. But if you grab hold of the promise in this Scripture, you know your end will *increase abundantly*. Your ministry, business, and life may be small today, but in your future you are much bigger than you are today. God has promised you a future that is bigger and better than your present.

You must learn to live big in the small place before the small place will ever become bigger. God is an expert at taking nobodies and making them somebodies. The worst days of your life are behind you, and the best days of your life are ahead of you. Mike Murdock said, "When you have nothing left but God, you have enough to start again."

I will never forget the time we went to a very small country church in Michigan. I thought to myself before I went into the sanctuary to minister, *What am I doing in this little place? I am going to preach a short sermon and get out of here.* Then the Holy Spirit rebuked me and said "Do not be negative about this small church. For I birth big people and big ministries in small places. You could be preaching to the next Kathryn Kuhlman, Benny Hinn, T.D. Jakes, or Joyce Meyer."

Think about this: God birthed a big, universal, creative ministry on a small planet called Earth. Then God chose a small manger to birth a big Man and a big redemptive ministry, Jesus Christ. God chose a small upper room to birth 120 big men and women into ministry. The impact of these ministries continue to touch people's lives even in the 21st century.

Many people do not want to start small. Therefore, they do not attempt to start anything new. You must realize that everything great started small. Every large business or church started small. Disneyland started with a mouse. The forest in your back yard started as a seed. The skyscraper began with one small brick. Every big dream started with a thought. God loves the start of new things. Why? Because starting your dream takes faith, and faith pleases God.

Do not despise this small beginning, for the eyes of the Lord rejoice to see the work begin...
—Zechariah 4:10 TLB

It is not wrong to be in a small place as long as you do not allow the small place to get inside you. God cannot increase your end abundantly as long as you have decrease or small living on your mind. What has your attention will have your direction. If decrease has your attention, you will naturally move toward decrease and lack. If increase has your attention, you will naturally move toward increase and abundance. God is a God of increase. He wants to increase you, *May the LORD give you increase more and more, you and your children* (Psalm 115:14). Increase means to have more than what you started with.

God Wants to Increase You

What does God want to increase or give you more of? He wants to give you more:

- ➲ Joy (John 15:11).

- ➲ Peace (Phil. 4:7).

- ➲ Wisdom (James 1:5).

- ➲ Wealth (Psalm 112:1-3).

- ➲ Greatness (Psalm 71:21).

- ➲ Seeds to sow (2 Cor. 9:10).

- ➲ Health and Healing (Prov. 3:1-2).

- ➲ Things (Matt. 6:33).

- ➲ People saved (Psalm 2:4).

- ➲ Knowledge about God (Col. 1:10).

- ➲ Benefits (Psalm 68:19).

God does not want to give you more debts and bills, a larger waist size, or more headaches in life. In order for you to live big in a small place, you must start thinking big, talking big, acting big, dressing big, and giving big while you are in the small place, before the small place will ever grow and increase.

Small thinkers don't get the big breaks. If you want to get richer, think bigger first.

—Robert Kiyosaki

Thinking Big

Your mind is a "thought factory" that is busy producing 50,000 thoughts in one day. One single thought has the power to change the entire world. Your thoughts are controlling where you are going in life. Everything that has been created has been started with a thought. Out of the abundance of a thought the creative process begins. Therefore, if small people can stop your thought life, they can destroy your creativity and even your destiny. This is why, although you may have nothing, you have to walk around with big thoughts. If your thoughts do not grow, nothing else in your life will grow. Your dream will never grow beyond your thinking capacity. You cannot create any further than you can think. Your capability to lead during times of crisis will be hindered.

All you need is one good thought to live like a king the rest of your life.

—Ross Perot

Thinking big thoughts while you are in the small places is the key to moving you out of the small place and beyond the current crisis. Little people have small thoughts in the small places, that is why they are small. I cannot change your future unless I can change the level of your thinking. What you are and where you are is the result of how you have thought and acted up to this point in your life.

You can find relief in worship but not be changed. You can find relief in a revival service but not be changed. You can even find relief by going to the mall shopping for the day. You can find relief in going to church every Sunday but not be changed. If you are going to change your life, you must change your thinking. Refusing to think small is your first step.

God's plans for your life are on a much larger scale than your plans or thoughts. Think about this: The universe was a thought in the mind of God before He spoke it into existence. Trust me, our God thinks BIG! Here we are on this little blue marble planet trying to grasp the thoughts and plans that God has for our lives. His plans for us go beyond what we could ever imagine or think. Fortunately, God works through our small minds. Let's look at what the Bible says about God's thoughts and our thoughts:

"For My thoughts are not your thoughts, nor are your ways My ways," says the LORD. "For as the heavens are higher than the earth, so are My ways higher than your ways, and My thoughts than your thoughts."

—Isaiah 55:8-9

But as it is written: "Eye has not seen, nor ear heard, nor have entered into the heart of man The things which God has prepared for those who love Him"

—1 Corinthians 2:9

Now to Him who is able to do exceedingly abundantly above all that we ask or think, according to the power that works in us.

—Ephesians 3:20

Make no mistake about it, you serve a God who is unlimited in what He can do for you and through you. It is time for you to take the limits off: 1) your God; 2) yourself; 3) your business; and, 4) your ministry. It's time for you to start dreaming and thinking big. You may not be accomplishing much because you are not expecting to accomplish very much.

Man's mind, stretched to a new idea, never goes back to it's original dimensions.

—Oliver Wendell Holmes

Your God has unlimited resources. The earth is the Lord's and all the gold and silver belongs to Him (see Psalm 24:1; Hag. 2:8). You limit God because you ask too small, think too small, and pray too small. Turn up your expectation level. Ask big, think big, and pray big prayers. You will not frighten God, trust me.

In Egypt, the Israelites depended on Pharaoh, or the world, to meet their needs. In the wilderness they learned to depend on God for their daily needs. Before they could enter into the Promised Land, they had to understand that the place of abundance depended on both God and man. What stopped the children of Israel from entering the Promised Land? It was not God, the devil, or the flooding of the River Jordan. It was the small thinking of the men, the leaders of Israel. Look what these leaders reported after they had spied out the Promised Land, *"There we saw the giants (the descendants of Anak came from the giants); and we were like **grasshoppers** in our own sight, and so we were in their sight"* (Numbers 13:33).

Which group of people do you think is harder to change— leaders or followers? The answer: leaders. Why? Because followers will go wherever a person leads them. If you can change the thinking of the leadership in any organization, you can change the church or company. The leader is the barometer of the people. If the leader thinks big, the people will think big. If the leader thinks small, the people will think even smaller. If the leader is negative, the people in the organization will also be negative.

If you think you are a grasshopper, you are. If you think of yourself as a loser, you are a loser. If you see yourself as a millionaire, you may become one. If you see yourself as a winner or a champion, you *will* be one. *"For as he thinks in his heart, so is he..."* (Proverbs 23:7).

There is a plaque on the office wall of golfer Arnold Palmer that reads:

If you think you are beaten, you are.
If you think you dare not, you don't.
If you'd like to win but think you can't,
It's almost certain you won't.
Life's battles don't always go
To the stronger or faster man,
But sooner or later, the man who wins
Is the man who thinks he can.

Joshua and Caleb saw themselves as being well able to conquer any giant who stood in their way. These two men saw themselves as champions. Look at what Caleb said about the Promised Land:

> *Then Caleb quieted the people before Moses, and said, "Let us go up at once and take possession, for we are **well able** to overcome it."*

> —*Numbers 13:30*
> (Emphasis Added)

Notice that Caleb says, "Let us go up at once!" Why did he make this statement? Because he knew that over a period of time the negative, small thinking people would try to talk them out of their Promised Land. Do not let anyone talk you out of your future. Refuse to allow tradition to paralyze your thinking. Be receptive to new ideas and be progressive in everything you do.

People are not measured by inches or pounds or college degrees or family background. They are measured by the size of their thinking. How big we think determines the size of our accomplishments.

—Source Unknown

When you are going against the flow of what everybody else is doing, you are going to face some resistance. Average people go with the flow, that is why they are just average. Many people go through life and never use their imagination. Some people use their imagination to cheat people out of money and for evil. It is time for God's people to use their imaginations for dreaming about their futures. Use your imagination to invent new ways of helping people and to create new solutions to problems in our world today. Your mind is a powerful tool that God gave you; it is time to start using it.

You are motivated to become what you have imagined yourself to be.

—Source Unknown

The purpose of your imagination is to show you the potential events or accomplishments of your future. You can never tap into your full potential unless you can imagine accomplishing something unusual in your future. Walt Disney said, "If you can dream it, you can do it." He imagined a huge theme park where families could go to have clean entertainment and fun.

A place where people could escape the hustle and bustle of life. Since Disneyworld and Disneyland opened, millions of people have poured into Florida and California from all over the world to relax and enjoy themselves.

The man who has no imagination has no wings.

—Muhammad Ali

People who think big thoughts will naturally attract big people. Big people are only drawn to others who think big thoughts and dream big dreams. Big people have the money to help you with your big dreams.

It is very important for local pastors to start thinking bigger about themselves. You need to see yourself as the pastor of the entire city, instead of the pastor of the 100-1,000 people you preach to on Sunday morning. You must start to think like a big church before you become a big church. Those who pastor large churches do not run around doing the menial tasks of the church. They train and equip others to do the work for them. When you train others to do the work of the ministry, you instantly multiply your potential.

It is time for God's people to start thinking big while they are in their small place. It is time for you to think about starting and owning your own business. Do not quit your regular job, but burn the midnight oil and start a business out of your house. While you are working for McDonalds, start thinking that one day you will own your own McDonalds. As long as you only see yourself as a cashier, that is all you will ever be.

You have to move up to another level of thinking, which is true for me and everybody else. Everybody has to learn to think differently, bigger, to be open to possibilities.

—Oprah Winfrey

When little people try to drive you down—*think bigger!* When non-achievers criticize you—*think bigger!* When you get discouraged—*think bigger!* When the odds are against you—continue to *think bigger!* When you start thinking bigger, you will naturally start talking bigger. The Bible says *"...For out of the abundance of the heart the mouth speaks"* (Matthew 12:34).

Talking Big in Small Places

Death and life are in the power of the tongue, and those who love it will eat its fruit.
— *Proverbs 18:21*

Your words are spiritual containers of creative or destructive power. You can use your words to build up a ministry or business or to tear it down. Words are energy producing or energy draining. Your words can be full of faith or fear, blessings or curses, positive or negative, victory or defeat, creativity or destruction, vision or division.

In your crisis, setback, or small place, you will need extra energy to more effectively move forward into your future. Your dream will require hours of planning and hard work. Speaking negative words reduces your energy level and slows down your progress. Speaking positively increases your energy level and increases your productivity. When you speak positive, affirming words about your life and future, you will eat the fruit of what you say.

When you talk small about the small place, the small place will continue to remain small. If you speak negatively about the small place, the smaller place will become even smaller.

Words create pictures. Say, "pink elephant." The minute you said pink elephant, you saw a picture of a pink elephant in your mind. In the same way, the words you speak can create pictures of winning or pictures of losing. Most Olympic champions can see themselves finishing in first place before they start the race.

Your words create pictures of where you want to be in the future. In the small place you must learn to talk big about tomorrow. It is easy to find people who will speak negatively about your present situation. Job's friends had many discouraging words for him when he faced his crisis. If you do not talk big about your future, nobody else will. You must make statements like, "Things might look bad this week, but next week is going to be better than this week." "We might be small now, but in five years we are going to be huge!" "Where are we going to sit all the people who are going to get saved?" "What are we going to do with all the millions our business makes?"

People who talk big have to remove "little" words from their vocabulary. These words are not found in an achiever's dictionary:

- Can't
- Impossible
- Unbelievable
- Hopeless
- Illogical
- Hard
- Afraid
- Failure

Acting Big in Small Places

Square your shoulders, hold your head up, and put a smile on your face. Start acting like you are important. You might say "But I'm a little nobody in my company." Well, you are not a little nobody in God's eyes! Think about it, out of the entire world, you were so special that God called you to be part of His Kingdom. You are part of a Kingdom that has no end. The Lord has made you a king and a priest in His Kingdom (see Rev. 1:6). That makes you important. Are you acting like a king or a peasant, a sinner or a priest? Don't expect to be treated like a king if you keep acting like a peasant.

If you want a big church, start acting like the small one is big. Big churches have organized greeters and ushers at the front door. Why should God give you a church with 25 entrances, when you can not properly greet visitors at one entrance? Big churches have ushers who look professional. Why should God trust you with more money when you can not properly organize the offering time? Why should God give you more money when you do not have offering baskets big enough to handle it all? Until you start acting like a big church, you will never become a large church.

If you work in the marketplace, you must start seeing yourself as the future boss, vice president, or CEO of the company you work for. Then start acting like a boss. Simply do what people in management positions do: 1) They come into work early; 2) They pick up paper on the floor; 3) They will usually have a good attitude about the company; 4) They work hard and go the extra mile.

People who never do any more than they get paid for, never get paid for any more than they do.

—*Elbert Hubbard*

Dressing Big in Small Places

All men are created equal, then they get dressed.

—Billboard

Your personal appearance is like a billboard that tells all about you. Yes, your appearance "talks." It is either saying positive or negative things about you. When you dress for success, you present an appearance of success, wisdom, and excellence. If you dress sloppily, you present an appearance of failure, ignorance, laziness, and sloppiness. People see what we are before they hear what we say. It's true that you will never get a second chance to make a good first impression.

Yes, God looks at the heart—but people judge our outward appearance. More than likely your boss or president of the company is not a "spiritual person." He or she is not praying that the Lord would reveal who to promote. Where you are will determine who sees you. If nobody sees you, the odds are that you will never be promoted. How you look when they do see you determines the amount of favor you receive.

Joseph shaved and changed his clothing before he went to see Pharaoh (see Genesis 41:14). This shows us that Joseph understood the secret of looking your best and dressing for success. Naomi told Ruth to, "...*wash yourself and anoint yourself, put on your **best garment** and go down to the threshing floor...*" (Ruth 3:3) before she presented herself to the rich young man named Boaz. Ruth found favor in Boaz sight and eventually became his wife.

I have met several single people who are struggling to find a mate. They have prayed and fasted but to no avail. My question to every single person: Do you really want to find a mate? Then stop praying so hard and start dressing nicely. Ladies, men are not turned on by your prayer life and your devotional life. Men are tuned on by sight. How do you expect to catch a man's attention if you do not even take the time to style your hair? Men, nothing turns women off more than a poorly groomed man. It is important that you wear cloths that match, brush your teeth, wear deodorant, get your hair cut on a regular basis, clean your fingernails, buff your shoes, and take a daily shower.

Dress like you want to be addressed.

—Archbishop Benson Idahosa

Queen Esther understood the secret of dressing for success. Look what she did to get the king's attention:

Now it happened on the third day that Esther put on her __royal robes__ and stood in the inner court of the king's palace, across from the king's house, while the king sat on his royal throne in the royal house, facing the entrance of the house. So it was, when the king saw Queen Esther standing in the court, that __she found favor in his sight__, and the king held out to Esther the golden scepter that was in his hand. Then Esther went near and touched the top of the scepter. And the king said to her, "What do you wish, Queen Esther? What is your request? It shall be given to you; up to half the kingdom!"

—Esther 5:1-3
(Emphasis Added)

Why did she find favor in his sight? What caught the king's attention? Make no mistake about it—Queen Esther was dressed for success!

If you see a woman wearing a wedding gown, you know she is going to a wedding. If you see another woman wearing a bathing suit, you know that she is headed for the beach. If you see a kid wearing a baseball uniform, you know he is headed to a baseball game. If you see a person wearing a clown costume, you know they are headed for the circus. If you see a man who is wearing a navy blue pinstriped suit, white shirt with a red tie, and carrying a briefcase, you know he is going to an important business meeting. The way you are dressed tells people where you are going.

Do not judge a book by its cover.

—Source Unknown

There have been many exceptional books written that had very poor sales to the public because the cover was poorly designed. There has also been thousands of terribly written books that experienced great sales because of an eye-catching cover design. Publishers will instruct you to spend extra money on the cover design of any book you may publish. You may be a very hard worker, intelligent, highly educated, a loyal worker, honest, and have great leadership abilities, but our natural human tendency is to judge people by their outward appearance. Therefore, if you don't put a "nice cover" on your body, people may perceive you as a "bad book."

Many people think that they have a right to dress the way they want and they do. However, there is a time to work, a time for leisure, and a time to play. Therefore, there is a time to dress for success (work), a time to wear your pajamas (leisure), and a time to wear shorts and a tank top (play). You can chose how you want to dress for leisure and play, but not for work—that is, if you want to be a success. How you look on the outside affects the way you feel on the inside. Looking important will help you think important, talk important, and act important.

Big Givers in Small Places

*And Jesus sat over against the treasury, and beheld how
the people cast money into the treasury: and many that were
rich cast in much. And there came a certain poor widow,
and she threw in two mites, which make a farthing. And
He called unto Him His disciples, and saith unto them,
Verily I say unto you, That this poor widow hath cast
more in, than all they which have cast into the treasury:
For all they did cast in of their abundance; but she of her
want did cast in all that she had, even all her living.*
—*Mark 12:41-44 KJV*

This story in Mark is of a woman who gave big while she
was in a small place. She did not have very much money. She
had obviously faced a major crisis or a temporary setback.
However, in her lack, or want, it was the percent of the widow's
giving that captured Jesus' attention. She gave 100 percent.
God is concerned about the percentage of what we give. People
get impressed by the amount. Many people in that day gave
very large amounts, but they gave a very small percent.

Do you think that Jesus actually let this woman walk out
of the temple that day without giving her some of His own
money? I believe He did. One thing I do know, after this widow
gave all she had, God moved Heaven and earth to see to it that
all her needs were supernaturally met.

The enemy keeping you from reaching the big place is
holding on to the small blessings, when God wants to get the
big blessings into your life. During one of our crusades in
West Virginia, I was teaching on the subject of obeying the
voice of the Lord in giving. A single woman testified that God
had instructed her to give $100 three nights in a row. She was

saving this money to buy a new car. For this single woman, $300 was a tremendous amount of money. She was obedient, and a short time later, her mother called and told her that she wanted to buy her a new $30,000 Jeep Cherokee. This single woman let go of the small blessing, so she could receive the big blessing that God had for her. Your outrageous giving in your present creates an outrageous harvest in your future.

Get Seed into the Soil for Your Future

There was a __famine in the land,__ besides the first famine that was in the days of Abraham.

—*Genesis 26:1*

Would you classify a famine in a country a crisis? Famine, inflation, and economic hard times have been with us since the beginning of time. This is not a new problem that demands a new solution. In the Book of Genesis, God gave Isaac a battle plan for surviving the crisis season that included two strategies: Obey God's commandments and His voice and give generously during a crisis.

Strategy 1—Obey God's Commandments and His Voice

Then the LORD appeared to him [Isaac] and said: "Do not go down to Egypt; live in the land of which I shall tell you."

—*Genesis 26:2*

Isaac was instructed by the Lord to stay in his present location. During this time of famine, everybody was going to Egypt for food. Egypt represents the "world system." Isaac was not allowed to follow the world's way of doing things. The

115

world system says, "If you are going to make it through tough times, you better save all the money you can. Whatever you do, do not give anything away." You are not to follow the world's philosophy, but instead God's way of doing things. Therefore, you must make sure that you pay your tithes (10 percent) and give offerings as the Lord leads you (see Malachi 3:8-12). Your tithe is a declaration of your independence from the world's economic system and a declaration of your dependence on the economy of God. Many famous and successful men in America's past began tithing early in life. Many of these companies are strong businesses to this day!

- ➲ John D. Rockefeller

- ➲ H.J. Heinz (Heinz Inc.)

- ➲ H.P. Crowell (Quaker Oats)

- ➲ J.L. Kraft (Kraft Co.)

- ➲ M.W. Baldwin (Baldwin Locomotive)

- ➲ William Wrigley (Wrigley's gum)

- ➲ M.S. Hershey (Hershey's chocolate)

- ➲ William Colgate (Colgate toothpaste)[1]

Strategy 2—Give Generously During a Crisis

Then Isaac sowed in that land, and reaped in the same year a hundredfold; and the LORD blessed him
—Genesis 26:12

Many people refuse to sow or give during a time of crisis. Why? A crisis creates fear. Isaac took control of his future by sowing a seed in his present. What he sowed that day went into his future and produced his desired outcome. In the middle of a crisis, Isaac found his entrance into a new season of change and abundance. Maybe you cannot change your present, but you can change your tomorrow.

Every seed has an invisible instruction. A corn seed has an instruction to produce a corn stock and an orange seed has an instruction inside to produce orange trees. Every seed has a germination process. This is a time in which the seed must stay in the soil and be watered. Then it will start to grow. Seed in the barn will not reproduce a harvest. Money under your mattress or in the bank will not produce a multiplied harvest.

Money seed sown into ministry will produce multiplied money. One dollar bills will produce ten and twenty dollar blessings. One hundred dollar offerings will produce thousand dollar financial blessings. Thousand dollar bills will produce ten and twenty thousand dollar blessings. The problem with most people in the church today is that they want ten and twenty thousand dollar blessings with one dollar bill seeds. In laymen terms, they want to sow one corn seed and reap an entire field of corn. One corn seed will not produce an entire field of corn. We are not responsible to complete a miracle, only to start one by sowing seeds. The time to start sowing seeds is when times are tough.

#1 Hindrance for Not Giving during a Crisis—Fear of Loss

Cast your bread upon the waters, for you will find it after many days. He who observes the wind will not sow, and he who regards the clouds will not reap.

—*Ecclesiastes 11:1,4*

Every seed that you plant, actually never leaves your life. Your seed goes toward your future to produce a desired harvest. Solomon was teaching us that if you look at your current crisis situation, you will not sow. Why? Because of your fear of loss. Fear is the feeling of anticipated loss. It may be the loss of a good reputation, property, money, love, health, or life. Fear is the enemy of faith. We are commanded not to fear or worry, *"Fear not, for I am with you; be not dismayed, for I am your God. I will strengthen you, Yes, I will help you, I will uphold you with My righteous right hand"* (Isaiah 41:10).

Those who observe their "natural" situations will live in fear and will not reap a supernatural harvest in their future. Fear causes many people to hoard during a time of crisis. This is the most unwise thing you can actually ever do. Why? Because a seed of nothing will produce a season of nothing. When you refuse to sow or give generously during a crisis, you destroy your own ability to expect a miracle in your future. Remember, a farmer can only expect a harvest after he has planted a seed.

When you decide to give big in the small place, you will unlock a spirit of expectation in yourself for a better tomorrow. Every time you give, you activate your faith. Every time you activate your faith, the seasons of your life start changing. When you activate your faith, you please God and you also torment the devil.

ENDNOTES_____

1. Perry Stone Jr., "Supernatural Provision in the End Times," *Voice of Evangelism* (1999), 46.

CHAPTER EIGHT

CRISIS: THE REMINDER THAT YOU HAVE AN ENEMY

On September 11, 2001, the United States of America faced one the greatest crises in its history as a nation. A small group of terrorists were successful in crashing commercial airliners into the twin towers of the World Trade Center and the Pentagon. This tragedy killed thousands of innocent people. How did a small group of terrorists effectively attack the most powerful country in the world? They surprised us. The element of a "surprise attack" has always been an effective military and enemy strategy. The largest armies in the world can be defeated and even destroyed if caught off guard when attacked.

A crisis will wake you up to the fact that you do have an enemy. A crisis is proof that the enemy believes you can accomplish your God-given dreams and goals.

Have you ever been in a place in your life where it seems as though everything around you is falling apart? You were praying, reading God's Word, praising the Lord, and giving your tithes and offerings, but nothing seemed to be working.

Have you ever felt like you were in a cycle of failure? Have you faced one setback only to find another obstacle around the corner? Do you sometimes feel like your future looks bleak and dismal? Have you ever asked the Lord, "Are You ever going to bring me my miracle," and "Am I ever going to get my breakthrough?" If you can relate to these questions, then hold on because help is on the way!

For almost two years of my life I struggled in a vicious cycle of shattered dreams, disappointments, discouragements, and financial struggles. After receiving another major blow in my ministry, I asked God for wisdom about how to break the cycle of defeat in my life. I was not ready to hear what the Lord was going to tell me.

I heard the Holy Spirit say, "When are you going to start taking control over your present situations and your future?"

My reply, "Lord, I have been asking You for a breakthrough for two years now."

Then the Lord said, "Why are you waiting on Me to bring about the changes? I gave you authority and seed so that you could control your own destiny. It is time for you to boldly take a stand against your adversary and the circumstances of your life."

Then the Holy Spirit led me to the following Scriptures:

*Behold, I give **you** the **authority** to trample on serpents and scorpions, and over all the power of the enemy, and nothing shall by any means hurt you.*

Luke 10:19
(Emphasis Added)

*And I will give **you** the **keys** of the kingdom of heaven,
and whatever **you** bind on earth will be bound in heaven,
and whatever **you** loose on earth will be loosed in heaven*

—Matthew 16:19
(Emphasis Added)

Satan has been Trying to Hide Your Position of Authority from You.

The Lord Jesus Christ has given you authority, which is the right to command. He has also given you power, which is the right to act. Nowhere in the New Testament are you told to pray to God and then He will take care of the devil for you. The Bible tells us to, *"**Resist** the devil and he will flee from you"* (James 4:7). Please notice that the devil will flee from *you*, not God. When you resist the devil, you do so by both your actions and your words. Again, God gave you authority, the right to command, and the power to act.

**Life does not give you what you deserve.
Life gives you what you demand.**

—Archbishop Benson Idahosa

You have been given the keys of the Kingdom. Keys denote authority. The transfer of responsibility has been given to you. Jesus gave you authority to bind (forbid) or to loose (permit) desirable outcomes on earth. Binding starts on earth first, then it will be taken care of by God in Heaven. We can ask God to do something for us all day long and never receive anything. Why? Because He gave *you* the right to rule over your own circumstances by accepting your God-given authority in Jesus' name.

In the beginning, God gave humankind two gifts: dominion and seed (see Genesis 1:26-29). If you want to reap a harvest of love, then sow seeds of love today. If you want financial and material blessings, then sow money and material things today. The seed you sow today, multiplies and goes into your future. Nothing "just happens." Your present condition is a direct result of what you sowed five-ten years ago. By sowing seeds, a person determines his or her own harvest for the future.

It takes more than just sowing seeds, though. Why? Because if you do not guard your field where your seed is being sown, a thief will come in and steal your seed. Satan and the world system are trying to rob you of your present seed so they can limit your future harvest. The question: What are you going to do about it?

You Were Created to Rule

A plane and a bird were created to fly. A fish was created to swim and a squirrel was created to climb trees. You were created to rule and reign in life!

*Then God said, "Let Us make man in Our image, according to Our likeness; let them have **dominion** over the fish of the sea, over the birds of the air, and over the cattle, over all the earth and over every creeping thing that creeps on the earth." So God created man in His own image; in the image of God He created him; male and female He created them. Then God blessed them, and God said to them, "Be fruitful and multiply; fill the earth and **subdue** it; have **dominion** over the fish of the sea, over the birds of the air, and over every living thing that moves on the earth."*

—Genesis 1:26-28
(Emphasis Added)

David was a man who walked in dominion. He made this statement about you, *"For You have made him* [humankind] *a little lower than the angels* [Hebrew-Elohim/God]*, and You have crowned him with glory and honor. You have made him to have **dominion** over the works of Your hands; You have put **all** things under his feet, all sheep and oxen; even the beasts of the field, the birds of the air, and the fish of the sea that pass through the paths of the seas"* (Psalm 8:5-8).

Adam was created in the image of God and after His likeness. God gave Adam dominion to rule over all the earth. He had been given dominion over everything that moved. The serpent moved. The Hebrew word for dominion is *radah* meaning to tread down, make to have dominion, prevail against, reign, make to rule or to take. What an awesome responsibility Adam had in the beginning. He became the king or the ruler of the entire earth.

The Fall from Glory

How did this powerful man of God fall? In the first place, Adam did not exercise his responsibility of lordship over the Garden of Eden. Look what the Bible says in Genesis 2:15, *"Then the LORD God took the man and put him in the garden of Eden to **tend** and **keep** it."* The Hebrew word for keep is actually "guard or protect." If Adam was to guard and protect the Garden, then he must have known that there was an enemy from which it needed guarded.

The very first crisis that happened in the Bible took place because Adam permitted the serpent to move into the Garden. America was viciously attacked by terrorists because we allowed the enemy into our country. Adam allowed the enemy in his house. Then the serpent tricked Eve, while Adam continued to twiddle his thumbs and did not take dominion over the devil. Adam could have said, "Devil you are a liar, get out of this Garden—now!" However, Adam did not walk in dominion and fell into sin.

The one who was called to rule now has to wear the devil's chains of slavery. Man either has dominion or he is under dominion. He cannot stay neutral. Man was created to be dominated by no force except for the divine. When man is not ruling, the effects can be devastating.

Rule Regained

After the fall of Adam, God initiated a plan to redeem humankind. God would send a Redeemer born through a virgin girl, who would bruise the devil's head, *"And I will put enmity between you and the woman, and between your seed and her Seed; He hall bruise your head, and you shall bruise His heel"* (Genesis 3:15). God sent His only begotten Son, Jesus Christ. Jesus paid the penalty necessary for our sins. Our Canon King then utterly defeated the devil for humankind, enabling every believer to daily walk in a place of divine dominion.

> *For if by the **one man's** offense* [Adam] **death reigned** *through the one, much more those who receive abundance of grace and of the gift of righteousness will **reign in life*** (reign as kings in life, AMP) *through the One, **Jesus Christ*** (Romans 5:17).

> *And raised us up together, and made us sit together* [sitting is a place of ruling and reigning] *in the heavenly places in Christ Jesus* (Ephesians 2:6).

You are seated in heavenly places with Christ Jesus. The position of sitting is a position of rulership. The word *dominion* in the New Testament usage means lordship, inherited rulership and sovereignty. Satan is currently crawling on his belly with a crushed head. Crawling on your belly in the dirt is not a place of rulership. The only thing you do to things that crawl is step on them. The only place your enemy belongs is under your feet.

I am here to take over, not to take sides. I have come to take over and I have no room for compromise. This is a whole new way of life; this is a whole new way of thinking. This is a whole new way of operation and when you get that settled, you're presenting the kingdom.

—*Bishop Eddie Long*

The Scope of Your Dominion

What do you have dominion over?

1. **You have dominion over sin.** *For **sin** shall not have **dominion** over you, for you are not under law but under grace* (Romans 6:14).

   You do not have to be controlled by any destructive sins or bad habits such as cigarettes, alcohol, drugs, over-eating, pornography, or gambling.

2. **You have dominion over your thought life.** *For the weapons of our warfare are not carnal but mighty in God for pulling down strongholds, casting down arguments and every high thing that exalts itself against the knowledge of God, bringing every **thought** into captivity to the obedience of Christ* (2 Corinthians 10:4-5).

   Your mind does not have to be a garbage container of negative thoughts. Your mind belongs to *you,* not the devil. Therefore, you have the right to control your own mind and to control your thoughts.

3. You have dominion over your emotions.
Finally, my brethren, be strong in the Lord and in the power of His might (Ephesians 6:10).

God would not tell you to be strong if you could not be strong. Your emotions will tell you to act weak and depressed. You can control your emotions by the power of the Holy Spirit.

4. You have dominion over sickness. *Then He called His twelve disciples together and gave them power and **authority** over all demons, and to **cure diseases*** (Luke 9:1).

You are God's property. Sickness and disease have no right to exist in your body.

5. You have dominion over demonic forces.
*Therefore submit to God. **Resist** the devil and he will **flee** from you* (James 4:7).

When a crisis takes the form of confusion, suspicion, and division, spiritual warfare is on. The ultimate success or failure of a disciple will not be in the visible realm but in the invisible realm. Just as science has moved activities to outer space, you must move your major activities to battle against the prince and power of the air.

6. You have dominion over nature. *But He said to them, "Why are you fearful, O you of little faith?" Then He arose and **rebuked** the winds and the sea, and there was a great calm* (Matthew 8:26).

The disciples could have done the same thing if they had exercised their faith and taken dominion over the storm.

In the Old Testament, Joshua stopped the sun and Elijah stopped the rain.

7. **You have dominion over your financial future.** *Do not be deceived, God is not mocked; for whatever a man sows, that he will also reap* (Galatians 6:7).

   You can control your own destiny by operating in God's law of seedtime and harvest. This starts with the tithe (see Malachi 3:8-12). If you are not tithing 10 percent of your income, you are opening the door for the devil to destroy your financial future.

8. **You have dominion over your family.** *Train up a child in the way he should go, And when he is old he will not depart from it* (Proverbs 22:6).

   You can control the destiny of your children if you will: Love them unconditionally. Discipline them. Train them.

What Destroys Dominion?

There are four things that will keep you from walking in dominion:

1. **Ignorance** - Hosea 4:6

2. **Unbelief** - Hebrews 3:19

3. **Sin** - John 8:34

4. **Refusing to submit to delegated authority** - Romans 13:1-2

America's hatred for those who commit terrorist attacks has increased since September 11, 2001. Why? Because we have experienced in our own country the evil of terrorism. In the heat of conflict, the Lord will increase your hatred for evil. Our hatred for evil should increase as we realize how the enemy has robbed us of our potential for achieving and enjoying what God has planed for us. Our hatred for evil should increase as we see how sin, unbelief, ignorance, and evil are damaging the lives of those we love. Learning to hate evil is the first step toward godly wisdom.

The fear of the LORD is to hate evil; pride and arrogance and the evil way and the perverse mouth I hate.

—*Proverbs 8:13*

The fear of the LORD is the beginning of knowledge, but fools despise wisdom and instruction.

—*Proverbs 1:7*

Kick the Enemy Out!

If it seems that evil will not depart from your household or church, it is possible that you have rewarded evil in some way, *"Whoever rewards evil for good, evil will not depart from his house"* (Proverbs 17:13).

Many people have treated those in the fivefold ministry very poorly. There are people in congregations worldwide who have talked badly about their pastors. Many preachers have treated traveling ministries poorly, and many traveling ministries have treated local church pastors poorly. When you treat badly those who have done nothing but good to you, you can reap a curse on your home and church.

The enemy usually attacks those who are next in line for supernatural promotion. He does not bother low-impact believers. The devil goes after big game. If you do not recognize when your crisis is nothing more than an attack from the devil, you will be overwhelmed and tempted to give up. A good soldier knows his enemy and prepares himself for battle. He must be skilled in the use of his weapons. Make no mistake about it, there is a real devil who has a real plan to get you to quit—to give up on your dreams and your God-given destiny. The enemy you are dealing with is satan and his demon spirits (see 1 Peter 5:8-9).

You will never reach the place where all opposition and attack will disappear. However, you are God's end-time warrior for the 21st century. You are armed and dangerous. You are carrying God's power and authority on earth. Satan and all His demons are subject to you. Stand up and boldly declare, "satan, take your hands off my marriage, my household, my family, my health, and my finances, in Jesus' name.

I love The Message Bible translation of James 4:7:

"Yell a loud NO to the devil and watch him scamper."

Conclusion

Leading in times of crisis can be rewarding as well as challenging. Whether you are leading your family, a community organization, a church group, or a Fortune 500 company, knowing the Source of your strength and peace gives you the victorious edge over the enemy and your circumstances.

From the truths, strategies, and promises of God shared throughout these pages, I have no doubt that, taken seriously, you will lead a triumphant life while on your journey to fulfill your God-given destiny.

Are you facing a crisis, trial, or setback?

You are not alone. I want to agree with you that God will supernaturally meet your needs.

Write your needs below and mail to:

Dr. Keith Johnson | P.O. Box 6777 | Spring Hill, FL 34611

Name

Address

City   State   Zip

Email

Need

Let's Get Connected ...

twitter.com/drkeithjohnson

facebook.com/drkeithjohnson

linkedin.com/in/drkeithjohnson

RESOURCES

The Destiny Arrow
Consulting Program

The *Destiny Arrow Consulting Program* is the ultimate program for those who demand the most out of life. As your consultant and coach I will serve you in two primary roles:

1. Leadership Coach

I will carefully consider your dreams, desires, and goals for the future, and help you create a customized blueprint using the strategic planning arrow to turn your dreams into reality.

2. Change Strategist

Every personal dream entails different levels with consequences of change. I will help you deal with the "fear of loss" in making the necessary changes you need to make to go to the next level and beyond. I will also help you develop a detailed step-by-step change strategy.

THE DESTINY ARROW!
Consulting Program includes:

➲ **INSTRUCTION**—You will be provided step-by-step instructions and training material.

➲ **WORKSHOP**—The Strategic Planning Arrow is a great team building tool that each member of your dream team will help you create in a one-day workshop setting. This process builds ownership of your vision and puts each team member on the same track to succeed.

⮑ **PERSONAL CONSULTATION**—You will receive guidance to sort through the fog and make your pathway crystal clear to reach your dreams and leave a lasting legacy.

Who uses and needs THE DESTINY ARROW! Consulting Program? The Strategic Planning Arrow is used daily by:

⮑ **ORDINARY PEOPLE** wanting to focus and plan their lives.

⮑ **LEADERS** starting their own organizations.

⮑ **PRESIDENTS** of major corporations.

⮑ **COLLEGE EDUCATORS**.

⮑ **PASTORS** of churches, large and small.

Engage THE DESTINY ARROW today!

To begin today, go to *www.LeadersofDestiny.com* for your initial evaluation. Or call **1-(888)-379-2663** to schedule an appointment. Or complete all the information on this form and send to:

The Confidence Coach | P.O. Box 6777 | Spring Hill, FL 34611.

Name	Title
Business Name	Website
Email Address	
Address	
City	State Zip
Office Phone	Cell Phone

Leaders of Destiny Coaching System

Destiny Arrow, Book, Manual, Training CD's

For more information visit:
www.LeadersofDestiny.com

THE CONFIDENCE MAKEOVER

How to Create the New and Confident You!

Confidence. Everybody wants it, but not everyone has it. More confidence allows you to reach your life potential and maximize your performance. Join Dr. Keith Johnson as he empowers you to quickly achieve higher levels of self-confidence so you can achieve the results you really want in life:

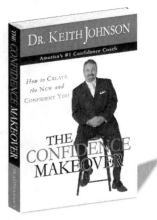

- ⮑ More Happiness!
- ⮑ More Money!
- ⮑ More Success!
- ⮑ More Power!
- ⮑ More Relationships!
- ⮑ More Fun!

Buy this new life-changing paperback book today! $19.99

For more information or to purchase this product, go to
www.TheConfidenceCoach.com
or call toll free:

1-(888)-379-CONFIDENCE
2 6 6 3

Confidence Coaching System

Maximize your confidence in only 30 days so you can:

⊃ Experience outrageous success in life.

⊃ Increase your happiness.

⊃ Double your income.

⊃ Fall in love with yourself.

⊃ Quickly change bad habits.

⊃ Speed up your destiny.

⊃ Create the amazing success you deserve!

The Confidence Coaching System empowers you to become a confident and successful person by recognizing your inner strengths and talents. Dr. Keith Johnson coaches you through a 30-day journey designed to reveal your potential and boost your best qualities. Drawing on the secrets of successful people, he shares easy-to-understand strategies that will maximize performance in every area of your life.

Order Online: *www.TheConfidenceCoach.com*
or call toll-free: **1-(888)-379-2663**

Stop Dreaming and Start Writing!

Dr. Keith Johnson's Writers' Boot Camp

There is a bestselling book hidden inside of YOU!

Do you dream of writing a book? Dr. Keith Johnson will show you how to take your dream of writing a bestselling book and make it a reality. Here are just a few secrets Dr. Keith reveals in this informative boot camp experience:

- ➲ How to take your book from an idea, to paper, to print.
- ➲ How you can become a multimillionaire selling information.

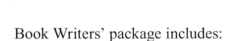

- ➲ 7 reasons why you need to write a book.
- ➲ How to use your book to get radio and television interviews.
- ➲ The "ins" and "outs" of obtaining an agent and publisher.
- ➲ How to get a publisher to accept your book.
- ➲ How to market your book to become a bestseller.
- ➲ And much more.

Book Writers' package includes:

- ➲ Teacher's Manual
- ➲ Student Manual
- ➲ 7 CDs recorded live at the conference

Cost: $149.00 (plus shipping and handling)

DR. KEITH JOHNSON
The Confidence Coach

Keith Johnson, The Confidence Coach, has spent the last 15 years successfully training over 120,000 leaders how to maximize their leadership potential and effectiveness.

- **Inspiring International Speaker**—Dr. Johnson is known as one of the premier speakers on the subjects of leadership and confidence building. He has spoken worldwide including in Japan, Singapore, Malaysia, Africa, Europe, India, and throughout the United States.

- **Frequent Television Guest**—He has shared his experiences on several major television and radio stations in America offering his expertise to help others become more confident and more successful..

- **Distinguished Author**—He has currently authored more than eight compelling books including *The Confidence Makeover*. He has authored numerous training manuals that provide practical and easy to understand and implement principles of confidence building.

- **Leadership Consultant**—He is known as a "change strategist" who coaches and serves leaders, empowering them to raise their organizations to the next higher level—and beyond.

- **Dedicated Learner**—Degrees earned: Master of Leadership and Doctor of Philosophy. Graduate of the Bobb Biehl Leadership Academy.

www.TheConfidenceCoach.com

> "Seeds of greatness are inside every human being. Sometimes it takes a crisis to expose them. Crisis forces you out of your comfort zone!"

—Dr. Keith Johnson
The Confidence Coach